Functional Architecture with React and Redux

Cristian Salcescu

Functional Architecture with React and Redux

Functional Architecture with React and Redux
Cristian Salcescu

Copyright © 2020 Cristian Salcescu

ISBN-13: 979-8607681111

History:

February 2020 First Edition

Contents

Preface	11
Fast Development Environment	13
Chapter 1: Introduction to the Functional Architecture	**15**
Pure Functions	15
Functional Architecture	15
State	16
View Functions	17
Actions	17
Update Functions	17
Immutable Data	18
Purity of the Unidirectional Flow	18
Final Thoughts	19
Chapter 2: View Functions with React	**21**
Function Components	21
Composing Components	22
React Elements	25
Virtual DOM and Rendering	25
JSX	26
Final Thoughts	26
Chapter 3: Update Functions with Redux	**29**
Store	29
Actions	30
Fibonacci Store	30
Final Thoughts	31
Chapter 4: Counter App	**33**

State	33
Actions	33
View Function	33
Update Function	35
Connecting	35
Entry Point	36
Final Thoughts	37

Chapter 5: Refactoring the Counter App — 39
Action Creators	39
Redux Actions	40
Mapping Events to Action Creators	40
Mapping Actions to Updaters	41
Final Thoughts	42

Chapter 6: Sidebar — 43
State	43
Actions	43
View Functions	43
Update Functions	45
Connecting	45
Other Views	46
Root View	47
Redux Dev Tools	47
Final Thoughts	48

Chapter 7: Color Search App — 49
State	49
Actions	49
View Functions	50
Update Functions	51
Selectors	52
Connecting	53
Testing	53
JSON	54
Entry Point	55
Final Thoughts	55

Chapter 8: Color Search App with Submit — 57
State	57
Actions	57

View Functions	58
Partial Application	58
Thunks	59
Connecting	59
Update Functions	60
Final Thoughts	61

Chapter 9: Loan Calculator App with Uncontrolled Inputs   63

State	63
Actions	63
View Functions	64
Form Submit Helpers	65
Form Validation	67
Update Functions	67
Selectors	68
Connecting	69
Root View	70
Final Thoughts	70

Chapter 10: Loan Calculator App with Controlled Inputs   71

State	71
Actions	72
View Functions	72
Update Functions	75
Final Thoughts	76

Chapter 11: Toast Notification Module   77

State	77
Actions	77
View Functions	77
Update Functions	80
Asynchronous Actions	81
Module	83
Other Views	83
Root View	84
Entry Point	84
Final Thoughts	85

Chapter 12: Weather App   87

State	87
Actions	87

Update Functions	87
API Utils	90
Promises	91
Operations	91
View Functions	92
Root View	94
Final Thoughts	95

Chapter 13: Hacker News App — 97

State	97
Actions	97
Update Functions	98
Selectors	98
API Utils	99
Operations	99
View Functions	101
Root View	103
Entry Point	103
Final Thoughts	103

Chapter 14: Show More Component — 105

State	105
Actions	105
View Function	105
Update Function	106
Root Update Function	107
Root View	107
Reusing the Update Function	108
Helpers	110
View Function with Local State	111
Final Thoughts	113

Chapter 15: NYT App — 115

Books	115
Fetching Data on Load	121
Higher-Order Components	122
Articles	124
Root Update Function	129
App Router	130
Entry View	130
AppRouter View	130

    Entry Point 131
    Final Thoughts 132

Chapter 16: Fetch Module   133
    State 133
    Actions 133
    Selectors 134
    View Functions 134
    Update Functions 135
    Operations 136
    NYT with the Fetch Module 137
    Final Thoughts 138

Chapter 17: Functional Architecture with React and Redux 141
    Decomposition 141
    Purity 142
    Side-Effects 142
    Folder Structure 144
    Final Thoughts 145

Preface

Functional programming is a programming paradigm aiming to make code easier to read, understand, debug and test.

We don't have to use a pure functional language to get the benefit of functional programming. We can get all these benefits using the first mainstream functional language, JavaScript, together with the most popular UI libraries, React and Redux.

We are going to experience the functional programming style by developing several applications with an incremental level of complexity. I encourage you to write all these applications yourself.

This book assumes you have a basic understanding of the JavaScript language and React library. If you are not confident about it, consider reading Discover Functional JavaScript and Functional React.

Source Code

The project files from this book are available at https://github.com/cristisalcescu/functional-architecture-with-react-and-redux.

Feedback

I will be glad to hear your feedback. For comments, questions, or suggestions regarding this book send me an email to cristisalcescu@gmail.com. Thanks in advance for considering to write a review of the book.

Fast Development Environment

The first thing we need to do is to set-up our development environment.

Package Manager

A package manager is a tool used to track project dependencies in an easy to use manner. At the time of writing, Node.js package manager, in short npm, is the most popular. Let's start by installing Node.js.

The following commands can then be used in command prompt to check the Node.js and npm versions:

```
node --version
npm --v
```

NPM Packages

With npm we can install additional packages. These packages are the application dependencies.

For example, here is the command for installing the Redux package:

```
npm install --save redux
```

The installed packages can be found in the node_modules folder. The --save flag tells npm to store the package requirement in the package.json file.

The package.json file stores all the node packages used in the project. These packages are the application dependencies. The application can be shared with other developers without sharing all the node packages.

Installing all the packages defined in the `package.json` file can be done using the `npm install` command.

Create React App

The easiest way to start with a React application is to use Create React App.

To do that, run one of the following commands:

`npm init react-app appname`

`npx create-react-app appname`

`npx` can execute a package that wasn't previously installed.

Once the application is created the following commands can be used:

- `npm start`: starts the development server.
- `npm test`: starts the test runner.
- `npm run build`: builds the app for production into the `build` folder.

IDE

For code editing, we need an Integrated Development Environment, IDE in short.

My favorite is Visual Studio Code.

To start the application, first, open the application folder in Visual Studio Code. Then open the terminal from Terminal→New Terminal and run: `npm start`. This launches the development server and opens the React application in the browser.

Chapter 1: Introduction to the Functional Architecture

Functional programming is a programming paradigm that promotes the use of pure functions and immutable values aiming to make reading and understanding an application easier.

Functional programming is to a large extent about data transformations. The focus is on writing pure functions that transform immutable data. These functions do not modify anything external to the function itself and should be small and simple.

Pure Functions

Pure functions are deterministic. Calling a function with the same input values returns the same result.

Pure functions have no side-effects, which means they do not modify the external environment or read data that can change from the outside environment.

Pure functions treat their arguments as immutable data.

Pure functions allow the reader to focus in one place, the current function and thus make code easier to read.

Pure functions don't have the `this` pseudo-parameter.

Functional Architecture

The emerging architecture for building frontend applications in a functional style is the Elm Architecture.

The application starts with an initial state. The state is then represented on the screen using the view functions. The user interaction with the view produces actions, which are handled by the update functions. The update functions transform the state based on these actions. The new state is then represented on the screen using the view functions. Once initialized the application executes this continuous loop. This is the unidirectional data flow.

Here is a sketch of the flow:

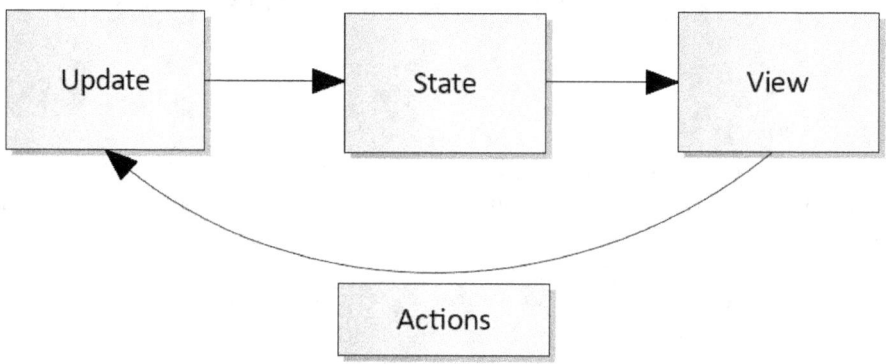

In summary, the common building blocks for creating an application in a functional style are:

- State, representing all the state of the application
- View functions, transforming the state into a visual interface
- Actions, expressing the user interaction
- Update functions, changing the state

State

The state is the data that is stored and can change over time.

The state value is immutable. Changing the state requires to create a new value.

The user interface is a reflection of the state. In order to change the user interface, we need to change the state. The state implies interactivity.

Let's consider the `book` object as the application state.

```
const book = Object.freeze({
  title: 'Beautiful Code',
  author: 'Douglas Crockford'
```

});

View Functions

The view functions transform the data into HTML and CSS.

React makes it easier to create view functions that take input data and return the visual representation of it using an HTML-like syntax called JSX.

Here is an example of a view function using the JSX syntax that transforms a `book` into HTML.

```
function BookView({ book }){
  return (
    <div>
      <div>{book.title}</div>
      <div>{book.author}</div>
    </div>
  )
}
```

The `BookView` function takes a `book` and creates a `<div>` element with two children containing the `title` and the `author`.

Actions

Actions are plain data objects used to express the user interaction.

They can be as simple as the following object:

```
{
  type: 'CHANGE_BOOK_TITLE',
  title: 'JavaScript The Best Parts'
}
```

Update Functions

The update functions transform the state. They receive the current state and an action and return the new state value.

Here is an example of an update function changing the `title` of a `book`.

```
function updateBook(book, action) {
  switch (action.type) {
```

```
    case 'CHANGE_BOOK_TITLE':
      return {
        ...book,
        title: action.title
      }
    default:
      return book
  }
}
```

The Redux library provides a functional approach for managing state using pure update functions.

Immutable Data

Immutable data is data that once created cannot be changed. Transforming immutable data requires to create new values. Instead of changing the original data we create changed copies.

The simplest way to make an object immutable is to use `Object.freeze()`.

Let's look at the book example.

```
const book = Object.freeze({
  title: 'Beautiful Code',
  author: 'Douglas Crockford'
});

const newBook = Object.freeze({
  ...book,
  title: 'How JavaScript Works'
});

console.log(newBook);
//{title: "How JavaScript Works", author: "Douglas Crockford"}
```

The spread properties syntax is used inside the object literal to copy all the properties of the `book` object into the newly created object.

Purity of the Unidirectional Flow

The view functions are pure functions. They take state data and return a visual HTML representation. Given the same input data, they return the same HTML code.

The view functions are not responsible for rendering HTML on a screen. React renders the HTML on the screen.

The update functions are pure functions. The update functions do not change the state directly. Redux uses the update functions to change the state.

Actions are plain immutable data objects.

All the state is read as an immutable value. Changing state requires to create a new value.

Final Thoughts

The state represents all the application data that can be changed. The state value is immutable.

The state is transformed into a visual interface using view functions.

The update functions change the current state based on the input actions.

React and Redux wires up the state, the view functions, and update functions.

The unidirectional flow implies getting the initial state, showing it to the user, listening for actions, updating the state based on those actions, and rendering the updated state back to the user again.

Chapter 2: View Functions with React

View functions transform data into a visual interface. In a web app, the visual interface is made of HTML and CSS.

React is a library for building user interfaces. The basic unit for a piece of the user interface is the component. React promotes the use of functions for declaring components.

In React the view functions are the function components.

Function Components

Here is an `Welcome` function component showing the `"Welcome!"` text.

```
function Welcome(){
  return <div>Welcome!</div>
}
```

The HTML-like code can be split over multiple lines for readability. In this case, it is recommended to wrap it in parentheses to avoid the problems with automatic semicolon insertion.

```
function Welcome(){
  return (
    <div>
      Welcome!
    </div>
  )
}
```

Function components take a single input called "props" and return a React element describing what should appear on the screen.

```
function Welcome(props) {
  return <h1>Welcome,{props.message}</h1>;
}
```

The destructuring syntax can be used inside the parameter list to extract properties from the **props** object.

```
function Welcome({message}) {
  return <h1>Welcome,{message}</h1>;
}
```

Note that the component name should start with an uppercase.

Composing Components

Components can refer to other components. For example, we can create the **App** component that uses the **Welcome** component:

```
function App() {
  return (
    <div>
      <Welcome message="The application has started" />
    </div>
  );
}
```

Let's take for example a simple Todo app.

We can start by creating a dummy **Header** view function.

```
import React from 'react';

function Header(){
  return <header>Header</header>
}

export default Header;
```

In a similar way, we can create the other **Footer**, **TodoSearch** and **TodoList** dummy view functions.

```
//Footer.jsx
import React from 'react';
```

```
function Footer(){
  return <header>Footer</header>
}

export default Footer;


//TodoSearch.jsx
import React from 'react';

function TodoSearch(){
  return <form>Search</form>
}

export default TodoSearch;


//TodoList.jsx
import React from 'react';

function TodoList(){
  return <div>List</div>
}

export default TodoList;
```

The `TodoView` view function can use the `TodoSearch` and `TodoList` view functions.

```
import React from 'react';
import TodoSearch from './TodoSearch';
import TodoList from './TodoList';

function TodoView(){
  return (
    <div>
      <TodoSearch />
      <TodoList />
    </div>
  )
```

}

export default TodoView;

Functions return only one element. Whenever we have multiple elements at the same level we need to wrap them into a parent element.

The **App** view function renders the interface using other three view functions.

```
import React from 'react';
import Header from './Header';
import TodoView from './TodoView';
import Footer from './Footer';

function App() {
  return (
    <div>
      <Header />
      <TodoView />
      <Footer />
    </div>
  );
}

export default App;
```

React apps have a single view at the very top called the root view. **App** is the root view in this example.

The practice is to split the page into smaller view functions and then compose those view functions back to create the page.

Splitting the page into small views creates a tree-like structure.

Here is the tree of views for the Todo app:

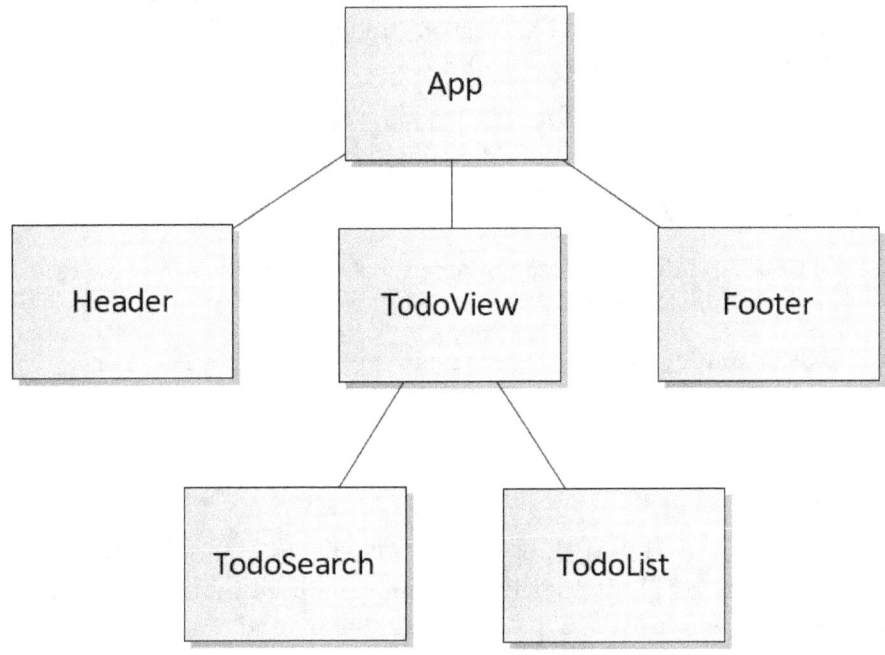

React Elements

React elements are plain objects describing what can be seen on the screen and are cheap to create.

React elements are immutable, once created they cannot be changed. The only way to update the UI at this point is to create a new React element.

Virtual DOM and Rendering

The real DOM is made of DOM elements. The virtual DOM is made of React elements.

The virtual DOM can be inspected using the React Developer Tools extension.

`ReactDOM` updates the DOM based on the React elements.

Changes to the virtual DOM are reflected in the real DOM in an efficient way. React updates the real DOM with only the necessary changes. Even if we create a React element describing the whole UI tree, only the necessary changes are applied to the real DOM.

`ReactDOM.render(element, containerDOM)` renders a React element, including all its children. The first argument is the React element, the second argument is the target DOM element.

React applications have a root DOM node where everything is rendered. Consider the following `app` DOM node:

`<div id="app"></div>`

The next code renders the React element created by the `App` view function into the `app` root DOM node.

`ReactDOM.render(<App />, document.getElementById('root'));`

JSX

The syntax used inside view functions is called JSX.

JSX is similar to HTML but is not HTML. JSX gets transpiled into JavaScript. Some HTML attributes cannot be used in JSX. For example, instead of `class` we need to use `className`, and instead of the `for` attribute we need to use `htmlFor`.

Expressions can be used inside JSX by wrapping them inside curly braces.

In the next example, the `message` variable is declared and used inside JSX.

```
function Welcome(){
  const message = "Welcome!";
  return <div>{message}</div>
}
```

JSX is converted to `React.createElement()` calls.

Final Thoughts

The simplest way to define a component is to write a JavaScript function.

Function components take all the inputs in an object called "props" and return React elements.

A React element describes what can be seen on the screen.

JSX defines React elements using a syntax similar to HTML.

The virtual DOM is a tree of React elements.

The `ReactDOM` library transforms the virtual DOM into the actual DOM.

React makes it easy to split the page into small view function components and then compose them together to create the whole page using JSX.

Splitting the views in smaller views creates a tree of views.

Chapter 3: Update Functions with Redux

The update functions take in the current state and an action and return the new state.

Redux manages the application state in a functional way using pure functions called reducers.

All the application state is stored in a single store object. The state can be read as an immutable object and changed only by dispatching actions. We can subscribe to state changes and update the user interface.

In Redux the update functions are the reducers.

First, in order to use Redux we need to install it.

```
npm install --save redux
```

Store

In an application there is a single store managing all the state.

The `createStore(reducer, initialState)` utility function creates the Redux store. It takes a single reducer function and an optional initial state value.

The `reducer` is a function that returns the new state value, given the current state tree and action to handle.

The store has just a few methods:

- `getState()` returns the current state tree of the application.
- `dispatch(action)` can change state by dispatching actions.
- `subscribe(listener)` allows listening for changes.

Actions

Actions are data objects with instructions about what should change in the application state. They contain the necessary data to make those changes.

Actions must have a `type` property that indicates the type of action being executed. Types are usually defined as string constants.

Fibonacci Store

Let's take the case of storing the current Fibonacci numbers and generating the next numbers in the sequence using a store.

State

The initial state, in this case, is made of the previous and current numbers in the sequence.

```
const initialState = Object.freeze({
  prevNumber: 0,
  currentNumber: 1
});
```

Actions

There will be only one action asking to generate the next number.

```
{ type: 'NEXT_FIBONACCI_NUMBER' }
```

Update Function

The update function handles the `NEXT_FIBONACCI_NUMBER` action by generating the new state.

```
function reducer(state = initialState, action){
  switch (action.type) {
    case "NEXT_FIBONACCI_NUMBER":
      return {
        prevNumber: state.currentNumber,
        currentNumber: state.prevNumber + state.currentNumber
      };
    default:
      return state;
```

```
    }
}
```

Update functions should always return something. When invoked with an unrecognized action the update function should return the current state.

Using the Store

We can now create the store using `createStore()` and then dispatch actions to change the state.

```
import { createStore } from 'redux';

const store = createStore(reducer);

store.subscribe(function(){
  const {currentNumber} = store.getState();
  console.log(currentNumber);
});

store.dispatch({ type: 'NEXT_FIBONACCI_NUMBER' });
//1

store.dispatch({ type: 'NEXT_FIBONACCI_NUMBER' });
//2

store.dispatch({ type: 'NEXT_FIBONACCI_NUMBER' });
//3

store.dispatch({ type: 'NEXT_FIBONACCI_NUMBER' });
//5
```

Final Thoughts

In essence, the Redux store keeps all the data as an immutable value that can be changed only by dispatching actions. Views can listen for these changes by subscribing to the store.

Actions are plain data objects describing the action to be performed.

Update functions handle actions by changing the state. Changing an immutable value means creating a changed copy.

32

Chapter 4: Counter App

Let's start implementing a simple counter. The app displays a counter on the screen and has two buttons for increasing and decreasing the number.

State

The state is just a number that is initialized with 0.

```
const initialState = 0;
```

Actions

When the + button is clicked the `counter` is increased. When the - button is clicked the `counter` is decreased. As a result, there are two action types:

```
const INCREMENT = 'INCREMENT';
const DECREMENT = 'DECREMENT';

export { INCREMENT, DECREMENT };
```

View Function

The `Counter` view function takes the `counter` number and creates the interface displaying it.

```
import React from 'react';

function Counter({counter}){
  return(
    <div>
      <div>{counter}</div>
      <div>
```

```
        <button type="button">
          -
        </button>
        <button type="button">
          +
        </button>
      </div>
    </div>
  )
}
```

`Counter` is a pure function.

The visual interface should allow dispatching actions based on user interaction. Let's do that by taking in two event handlers for incrementing and decrementing the `counter`.

```
function Counter({counter, onDecrement, onIncrement}){
  return(
    <div>
      <div>{counter}</div>
      <div>
        <button
          type="button"
          onClick={onDecrement}>
          -
        </button>
        <button
          type="button"
          onClick={onIncrement}>
          +
        </button>
      </div>
    </div>
  )
}
```

Handling events in JSX is similar to handling events on DOM elements, however React events are named using camelCase and the event handler function is assigned inside curly braces:

```
<button onClick={onDecrement} />
```

`Counter` is still a pure function. The view function defines the callbacks to be executed when the user clicks the buttons, it does not execute these callbacks. React uses the pure view function to render the interface and handles the user interaction by executing callbacks. The impure part is encapsulated by the React library.

Update Function

The update function transforms the state.

When it gets the `INCREMENT` action the update function increments the counter. When it gets the `DECREMENT` action the update function decrements the counter.

```
function reducer(counter = initialState, action){
  switch(action.type){
    case INCREMENT:
      return counter + 1;
    case DECREMENT:
      return counter - 1;
    default:
      return counter;
  }
}

export default reducer;
```

Connecting

The simplest way to connect the view functions to the store is to use the react-redux library.

`npm install react-redux --save`

In essence view functions read data from the store, and dispatch actions to the store. For this, we can use the `connect()` utility function.

`connect()` takes two functions as arguments:

- `mapStateToProps()` selects the part of the state that the connected view needs.
- `mapDispatchToProps()` dispatches actions to the store. It gets the `dispatch()` function as an argument and returns an object mapping

props to `dispatch()` calls.

```
import { connect } from 'react-redux';
import { INCREMENT, DECREMENT } from './reducer';

function Counter({counter, onDecrement, onIncrement}){
  //Code
}

function mapStateToProps(counter){
  return {
    counter
  }
}

function mapDispatchToProps(dispatch){
  return {
    onDecrement(){
      dispatch({ type: DECREMENT });
    },
    onIncrement(){
      dispatch({ type: INCREMENT });
    }
  }
}

export default connect(
  mapStateToProps,
  mapDispatchToProps
)(Counter)
```

The `mapStateToProps()` function takes the state as the `counter` parameter and sends it to the `Counter` view.

The `mapDispatchToProps()` function creates and dispatches the { type: INCREMENT } action on the `onIncrement` event and the { type: DECREMENT } action on the `onDecrement` event.

Entry Point

The `index.js` is the application entry point.

Here the Redux store is created and initialized with the update function.

```
import React from 'react';
import ReactDOM from 'react-dom';
import { createStore } from 'redux';
import { Provider } from 'react-redux';
import Counter from './Counter';
import reducer from './reducer';

const store = createStore(reducer);

const rootElement = document.getElementById('root')
ReactDOM.render(
  <Provider store={store}>
    <Counter />
  </Provider>,
  rootElement
)
```

The `<Provider />` component makes the Redux `store` available to all nested connected views. All the nested views inside the `<Provider />` component can be transformed into connected views using the `connect()` utility.

Notice that the code in the entry point is impure as it accesses the DOM.

Final Thoughts

The state for a simple Counter app is a number.

The `Counter` view function creates the UI displaying a number.

The update function increments or decrements the number depending on the action it receives.

All the functions written so far are pure. The only impure code stays in the application entry point.

Chapter 5: Refactoring the Counter App

There are a few things we can improve in the Counter App. For example, we can use action creators with the `connect()` utility function, or we can try to find a better option for mapping actions to state updates.

Action Creators

Actions are plain data objects. Here is the action used to increment the counter:

```
//action type
const INCREMENT = 'INCREMENT';

//action
{
  type: INCREMENT
}
```

Action creators are functions that create actions.

The action creators for incrementing and decrementing the counter may look like this:

```
function increment(){
  return {
    type: 'INCREMENT'
  }
}

function decrement(){
```

```
    return {
      type: 'DECREMENT'
    }
}
```

They are just pure functions returning plain objects.

Redux Actions

We can simplify the making of action creators using helpers. One option for this is the redux-actions library.

```
npm install --save redux-actions
```

The `createAction()` utility can be used to define the previous action creators.

```
import { createAction } from 'redux-actions';

const increment = createAction('INCREMENT');
const decrement = createAction('DECREMENT');

export { increment, decrement };
```

Mapping Events to Action Creators

Now we can use the `connect()` utility to map event handlers to action creators.

Below is the `Counter` view function using the `increment()` and `decrement()` callbacks as event handlers.

```
import React from 'react';

function Counter({counter, increment, decrement}){
  return(
    <div>
      <div>{counter}</div>
      <div>
        <button
          type="button"
          onClick={decrement}>
          -
        </button>
```

```
      <button
        type="button"
        onClick={increment}>
          +
      </button>
    </div>
  </div>
  )
}
```

connect() can take the second argument as a map. In this case, it uses the action creators to build the action objects and then dispatches those objects.

Below we are mapping the increment() and decrement() callbacks to the increment() and decrement() action creators.

```
import { connect } from 'react-redux';
import { increment, decrement } from './actions';

export default connect(
  mapState,
  { increment, decrement }
)(Counter)
```

As a shorter alternative, we can use mapState instead of mapStateToProps and mapDispatch instead of mapDispatchToProps.

Mapping Actions to Updaters

Functions should be small and do one thing. The switch inside the update functions leads to large code doing multiple things.

We can replace the switch with a map making the connection between actions and smaller update functions.

```
import { handleActions } from 'redux-actions';
import * as actions from './actions';

const initialState = 0;

//updaters
function increment(counter){
  return counter + 1;
```

}

```
function decrement(counter){
  return counter - 1;
}

export default handleActions({
    [actions.increment]: increment,
    [actions.decrement]: decrement
  },
  initialState
);
```

`increment()` increases the counter. `decrement()` decreases the counter.

When the `increment` action is dispatched, the `increment()` update function is executed.

When the `decrement` action is dispatched, the `decrement()` update function is executed.

`handleActions()` is a utility function from `redux-actions` that can map actions to smaller update functions and create a single update function handling multiple actions.

Final Thoughts

The `redux-actions` library can be used to simplify the making of action creators.

In connected views event handlers can be mapped to action creators.

Actions can be mapped to smaller update functions using a helper.

Chapter 6: Sidebar

Next, we are going to create a sidebar. Clicking the close button will collapse the sidebar. Clicking the show button will open it. We should be able to toggle the sidebar also from the outside its visual interface.

State

We need to know if the sidebar is opened or closed. The state can be just a boolean value.

```
const initialState = false;
```

Actions

We are going to use only one action, the one for toggling the sidebar.

```
import { createAction } from 'redux-actions';

const toggleSidebar = createAction('TOGGLE_SIDEBAR');

export { toggleSidebar };
```

View Functions

The `Sidebar` view function displays an opened or closed sidebar. To make things easier to understand we can create two other view functions for displaying these two cases.

The `SidebarOpened` view renders an opened sidebar.

```
function SidebarOpened({toggleSidebar, children}){
  return (
    <div>
```

```
      <button
        onClick={toggleSidebar}>
          &lt;
      </button>
      <div>
        {children}
      </div>
    </div>
  )
}
```

The `children` input property is used to display the HTML content passed to the component between the opening and closing tags.

Here is an example of invoking the component with content inside its tags:

`<SidebarOpened>This is the content.</SidebarOpened>`

All content inside the `<SidebarOpened>` tag gets passed into the component as the `children` prop.

The `SidebarClosed` view renders a closed sidebar.

```
function SidebarClosed({toggleSidebar}){
  return (
    <div>
      <button
        onClick={toggleSidebar}>
          &gt;
      </button>
    </div>
  )
}
```

Now, we can use these two view functions inside the `Sidebar` view and render only one of them, depending on the `show` property. This is called conditional rendering.

```
import React from 'react';

function Sidebar({show, children, toggleSidebar}){
  return(
    <div>
      {show?(
```

```
        <SidebarOpened
         toggleSidebar={toggleSidebar}
         children={children}
        />
      ):(
        <SidebarClosed
         toggleSidebar={toggleSidebar}
        />
      )}
    </div>
  )
}
```

Conditional rendering can be implemented with both the conditional operator and the `if` statement. In functional programming, we favor the conditional operator as it is an expression and always returns a value. The `if` statement does not necessarily return a value.

Update Functions

When the `toggleSidebar` action is dispatched, the `toggleSidebar()` update function runs and toggles the boolean value.

```
import { handleActions } from 'redux-actions';
import * as actions from './actions';

//updaters
function toggleSidebar(show, action){
  return !show;
}

export default handleActions({
    [actions.toggleSidebar]: toggleSidebar
  },
  initialState
);
```

Connecting

The `Sidebar` view reads the state as a boolean value and dispatches the `toggleSidebar` action.

```
import { connect } from 'react-redux';
import { toggleSidebar } from './actions';

function mapState(show){
  return {
    show
  }
}

export default connect(
  mapState,
  { toggleSidebar }
)(Sidebar);
```

Other Views

We can dispatch actions affecting the sidebar from other views.

Consider the `OtherView` view rendering a button calling the `toggleSidebar()` callback.

```
import React from 'react';

function OtherView({toggleSidebar}){
  return(
    <div>
      <button
        type="button"
        onClick={toggleSidebar}>
          Toggle
      </button>
    </div>
  )
}
```

Connecting

We can define the `toggleSidebar()` callback as a function dispatching the `toggleSidebar` action and thus toggling the sidebar from the outside its visual interface.

```
import { connect } from 'react-redux';
```

```
import { toggleSidebar } from './sidebar/actions';

export default connect(
  null,
  { toggleSidebar }
)(OtherView);
```

Root View

The `App` root view function renders the interface using the `OtherView` and Sidebar views.

```
import React from 'react';
import OtherView from './OtherView';
import Sidebar from './Sidebar';

function App() {
  return (
    <div>
      <OtherView />
      <Sidebar>This is the content.</Sidebar>
    </div>
  );
}

export default App;
```

Redux Dev Tools

To better analyze the flow inside an application, we should install the Redux Dev Tools. This requires to install a browser extension and to add a few lines of code when creating the store in the application entry point. Here is an example:

```
const store = createStore(
  reducer,
  window.__REDUX_DEVTOOLS_EXTENSION__ &&
  window.__REDUX_DEVTOOLS_EXTENSION__()
);
```

Final Thoughts

The special `children` property can be used to display the content included between the opening and closing tags when invoking a view.

Conditional rendering is the ability to render only some views depending on the application state.

Actions can be dispatched from any view.

Chapter 7: Color Search App

The Color Search App allows the user to find the color hex code. It uses a JSON file containing an array of color objects, each object having a name and a hex code.

Let's identify the parts of the unidirectional data flow.

State

There are two things we need to store, the list of colors and the current search term.

```
const intialState = Object.freeze({
  list: [],
  searchTerm: ''
});
```

Actions

We are going to use two actions one for setting the list of colors and another one for changing the current search term.

```
import { createAction } from 'redux-actions';

const setList = createAction('SET_LIST');
const changeSearch = createAction('CHANGE_SEARCH');

export { setList, changeSearch };
```

View Functions

The `ColorSearch` view function shows a form with the current search text. Changing the search term results in a call to the `changeSearch()` callback.

```
import React from 'react';

function ColorSearch({searchTerm, changeSearch}){
  return (
    <form>
      <input
        type="text"
        value={searchTerm}
        onChange={e => changeSearch(e.target.value)}
      />
    </form>
  )
}
```

Input updates are captured with the `onChange` event. `onChange` fires on each keystroke, not only on lost focus. In the `event` object, `event.target.value` gives access to the current value.

An input with both the value and the `onChange` properties defined is a controlled input. It displays the value and takes a callback function for changing that value.

The `ColorList` view builds the visual interface for a list of books. Let's start by creating the interface for an item.

The `ColorItem` view defines the interface for a single item in the list.

```
import React from 'react';

function ColorItem({color}){
  return (
    <div>
      <div>{color.name}</div>
      <div>{color.hexString}</div>
    </div>
  )
}
```

The same way we use `map()` to transform a list of values into another list of values, we can use `map()` to transform a list of values into a list of React elements.

The `ColorList` view function uses the `ColorItem` view to render the list of colors.

```
function ColorList({list}){
  return (
    <div>
      { list.map(color =>
          <ColorItem
            color={color}
            key={color.colorId} /> )
      }
    </div>
  )
}
```

The Item Key

The `key` is a special attribute that is required in a list of elements. It helps the React diff algorithm to decide what DOM elements to update. Each item in a list should have a unique identity defined by the `key` attribute. Usually, we are going to use ids as keys.

Keys are useful only when rendering a list. The `key` should be kept on the `<ListItem />` elements in the array and not in the `ListItem` view itself.

Keys are not passed to components. When we need the same value in the component we need to pass it in a property with a different name.

Update Functions

The update function handles the `setList` and `changeSearch` actions by just updating the current state with the new values.

The actual data of an action created with the createAction() utility is held in the `payload` property.

```
import { handleActions } from 'redux-actions';
import * as actions from './actions';

//updaters
```

```
function setList(state, action){
  return {
    ...state,
    list: action.payload
  }
}

function changeSearch(state, action){
  return {
    ...state,
    searchTerm: action.payload
  }
}

export default handleActions({
    [actions.setList]: setList,
    [actions.changeSearch]: changeSearch
  },
  intialState
);
```

Selectors

A selector is a function that accepts all the state as an argument and returns parts of that data or computes derived values from it.

`filterList()` extracts the color list and the search term from the state and returns a new filtered list.

```
function filterList({list, searchTerm}){
  return list.filter(color => containsName(color, searchTerm))
}

function containsName(color, searchTerm){
  return color.name
    .toLowerCase()
    .includes(searchTerm.toLowerCase());
}

export { filterList };
```

It is important to note that all the information needed by the selector has to be in the store. The selector does not have access to actions.

Connecting

The `ColorSearch` view reads the `searchTerm` from the store and dispatches the `changeSearch` action.

```
import { connect } from 'react-redux';
import { changeSearch } from './actions';

function mapState({searchTerm}){
  return {
    searchTerm
  }
}

export default connect(
  mapState,
  { changeSearch }
)(ColorSearch);
```

The `ColorList` view reads the filtered list of books from the store using the `filterList()` selector.

```
import { connect } from "react-redux";
import { filterList } from './selectors';

function mapState({list, searchTerm}){
  return {
    list : filterList({list, searchTerm})
  }
}

export default connect(mapState)(ColorList);
```

Testing

Unit tests allow detecting bugs and finding problems early in the development process. Unit tests cannot catch every error in the program but they may reduce uncertainty regarding the behavior units.

Projects created with Create React App have the Jest testing framework installed. We can simply define test files in the application by creating files named with the .test.js suffix.

The npm test command executes the tests.

Testing the Selector

Here is a simple test for verifying the search by color-name.

```
import { filterList } from './selectors';

test('filterList', function(){
  const list = [{
    "hexString": "#000000",
    "name": "Black"
  },
  {
   "hexString": "#800000",
   "name": "Maroon"
  }];

  const searchTerm = "black";

  const expectOutput = [{
    "hexString": "#000000",
    "name": "Black"
  }];

  expect(filterList({list, searchTerm})).toEqual(expectOutput);
});
```

The test() function defines a test block. Inside the test, we assert our expectations using the expect() function.

expect() returns an expectation object.

The toEqual() method can be called on the expectation object to test the value for equality. toEqual() recursively checks every field of an object or array.

JSON

Colors are stored in a JSON file.

JSON stands for JavaScript Object Notation. JSON is a lightweight format for storing and transporting data.

The JSON format is very similar to the code for creating JavaScript objects, and as such can easily be converted into native JavaScript objects.

The JSON format is text only.

Here is a sample from a JSON file used to stored colors:

```
[
  {
    "colorId": 0,
    "hexString": "#000000",
    "name": "Black"
  },
  {
    "colorId": 1,
    "hexString": "#800000",
    "name": "Maroon"
  }
]
```

Entry Point

When the application starts, all the colors from the JSON file are read and then dispatched to the store using the `setList` action.

```
import { createStore } from "redux";
import reducer from './reducer'
import colors from './colors.json';

const store = createStore(reducer);
store.dispatch(actions.setList(colors));
```

Final Thoughts

Controlled inputs are inputs with both the value and the `onChange` properties defined.

List components create the visual interface for a list of values. It is a good practice to extract out each item from the list into its own component.

Selectors are functions that retrieve and transform specific pieces of the state.

Unit tests can verify the functionality of pure functions in insolation. Tests can be defined in files with the `.test.js` suffix.

Chapter 8: Color Search App with Submit

When changing the text in the search text box, the color list is filtered. Let's add a search button and filter the color list only when the button is pressed.

State

This change requires to store two pieces of information, the current text in the textbox input and the search text used to filter the list of colors when the button is clicked.

```
const intialState = Object.freeze({
  list: [],
  searchTermInput: '',
  searchTerm: ''
});
```

Actions

We need a new action for updating the state when the search button is clicked.

```
import { createAction } from 'redux-actions';

const changeSearch = createAction('CHANGE_SEARCH');
const submitSearch = createAction('SUBMIT_SEARCH');

export { changeSearch, submitSearch };
```

View Functions

The `ColorSearch` view function invokes the `changeSearch` callback when the search textbox changes, and the `submitSearch` callback when the search button is clicked.

```
import React from 'react';

function ColorSearch({searchTerm, changeSearch, submitSearch}){
  return (
    <form>
      <input
        type="text"
        value={searchTerm}
        onChange={e => changeSearch(e.target.value)}
      />

      <button
        type="button"
        onClick={() => submitSearch(searchTerm)}>
          Search
      </button>
    </form>
  )
}
```

The click event is handled by an anonymous function executing the submit callback with the `searchTerm`.

Partial Application

Partial application is the process of applying a number of arguments to a function and creating a new function with fewer arguments.

We can do partial application using the `partial()` utility function from a functional library like lodash.

```
npm install lodash --save
```

`partial()` creates a version of the function that takes fewer arguments than the original function.

Partial application can be used to create the handler for the search click.

```
import partial from 'lodash/partial';

<button
 type = "button"
 onClick={partial(submitSearch, searchTerm)}>
   Search
</button>
```

The `submitSearch()` callback will be mapped to the action creator function expecting one argument, the `searchTerm`.

`partial(submitSearch, searchTerm)` returns a new function with the `searchTerm` argument already applied.

Thunks

A thunk is a function that delays the invocation of another function. The thunk function calls the original function with all the arguments.

`thunkify(f)` takes a function `f` and returns a new function that asks for arguments and returns a third function that, when called, invokes `f` with the all arguments.

In essence `thunkify()` returns a function that creates thunks. Such a function is available in the thunkify library.

`npm install thunkify --save`

Bellow is the submit handler rewritten with the `thunkify()` utility.

```
import thunkify from 'thunkify';

<button
 type="button"
 onClick={thunkify(submitSearch)(searchTerm)}>
   Search
</button>
```

Connecting

The `ColorSearch` view now dispatches two actions, `changeSearch` and `submitSearch`.

It reads the `searchTermInput` from the store and uses it to set the search input value.

```
import { connect } from 'react-redux';
import { changeSearch, submitSearch } from './actions';

function mapState({searchTermInput}){
  return {
    searchTerm: searchTermInput
  }
}

export default connect(
  mapState,
  {changeSearch, submitSearch}
)(ColorSearch);
```

Update Functions

The update function needs to handle both the `changeSearch` and `submitSearch` actions.

`changeSearch()` updates the search input value.

`submitSearch()` updates the search term.

```
import { handleActions } from "redux-actions";
import * as actions from "./actions";

//updaters
//code

function changeSearch(state, action){
  return Object.freeze({
    ...state,
    searchTermInput: action.payload
  })
}

function submitSearch(state, action){
  return Object.freeze({
    ...state,
    searchTerm: action.payload
  })
}
```

```
export default handleActions({
    //code
    [actions.changeSearch]: changeSearch,
    [actions.submitSearch]: submitSearch
  },
  intialState
);
```

Final Thoughts

Adding a Search button requires to save both the current input value and the searched value.

Partial application transforms a function with several arguments into a function with fewer arguments.

Applying the arguments on a thunkified version of a function does not execute the function but creates a thunk function executing the original function with all the arguments.

Chapter 9: Loan Calculator App with Uncontrolled Inputs

The Loan Calculator App displays a form with the amount required, the loan term in years, the interest rate per year and computes the total interest to pay.

State

The state is made of all the information the user has to enter. In this case, it is a good idea to initialize the state with the values for a common loan request.

```
const initialState = Object.freeze({
  amount: 10000,
  term: 5,
  interest: 5
});
```

Actions

In the loan form we need an action for the loan computation.

```
import { createAction } from 'redux-actions';

const submitLoanRequest = createAction('SUBMIT_LOAN_REQUEST');

export { submitLoanRequest };
```

View Functions

The `LoanResult` view function displays the information about the computed loan.

```
import React from 'react';

function LoanResult({ loan }){
  return(
   <div>
     <div>Total Interest Paid: {loan.totalInterest}</div>
     <div>Total Amount Paid: {loan.totalPaid}</div>
   </div>
  )
}
```

The `LoanForm` view collects the user input for a loan computation.

Forms are defined using input elements inside the `<form>` element. We are going to use uncontrolled inputs. Uncontrolled inputs do not have the value or the `onChange` callback defined, however, we can set the default with the `defaultValue` attribute.

```
import React from 'react';

function LoanForm({ loanRequest, submitLoanRequest }){
  return(
  <form>
    <div>
      <label htmlFor="amount">Loan amount</label>
      <input
        name="amount"
        type="number"
        defaultValue={loanRequest.amount}
        required
      />
    </div>
    <div>
      <label htmlFor="term">Loan term in years</label>
      <input
        name="term"
        type="number"
        defaultValue={loanRequest.term}
```

```
          required
        />
      </div>
      <div>
        <label htmlFor="interest">Interest rate per year</label>
        <input
          name="interest"
          type="number"
          defaultValue={loanRequest.interest}
          required
        />
      </div>
      <div>
        <button type="submit" >
          Calculate
        </button>
      </div>
    </form>
  )
}
```

We can handle the submit action by adding a submit button and a handler for the `onSubmit` event on the `<form>` element. In order to read the values from multiple inputs we need to add the `name` attribute to each input element.

The submit handler can be created with a helper.

Form Submit Helpers

A submit button is a `<button>` or an `<input>` element with the type `submit`. The default behavior of a form with a submit button is to submit the form data to the server and reload the HTML page.

We want to execute logic on form submit without reloading the HTML page.

preventDefault()

The `preventDefault()` method can be used on the `event` object to prevent the form from actually being submitted. We can encapsulate this call in a helper.

```
function preventDefault(e){
  e.preventDefault();
  return e
}

export { preventDefault };
```

FormData

The submit event allows accessing all the input values from the **event** object. We can use the FormData object to extract these values into a set of key/value pairs.

The following `extractFormData(e)` helper gets the submit event object and returns a map with all input values. Inputs need to have the **name** attribute in order for the helper to work.

```
function extractFormData(e){
  const formData = new FormData(e.target);
  const object = {};
  formData.forEach(function(value, key){
    object[key] = value;
  });

  return Object.freeze(object);
}

export {extractFormData};
```

pipe()

`pipe()` combines several functions into a pipeline where the output of each function is the input of the next one.

We can use `pipe()` to create the submit handler as a pipeline. It first prevents the default behavior, then it creates a map of name-value pairs and in the end, it calls the submit loan callback with this map.

The `pipe()` utility function can be found in library like lodash for example.

```
import pipe from 'lodash/flow';
import { preventDefault, extractFormData } from './helpers';
```

```
<form
 onSubmit={pipe(
   preventDefault,
   extractFormData,
   submitLoanRequest)}>
 ...

 <button
  type="submit">
    Calculate
 </button>
</form>
```

Form Validation

The simplest way to validate a form is with HTML5 validation attributes. The basic attributes for this are: `type`, `pattern`, and `require`.

The `type` attribute indicates what kind of input control to display, such as `"text"` for simple text data, `"number"` for validating numbers, `"email"` for a valid email address, or `"url"` for URLs.

The `required` attribute makes an input mandatory. The form will not submit and will display an error message when the input is empty.

The `pattern` attribute specifies a Regular Expression that the input value should match.

Update Functions

The update function handles the `submitLoanReques` action by updating the state with the new loan request values.

```
import { handleActions } from 'redux-actions';
import * as actions from './actions';

//updaters
function submitLoanRequest(state, action){
  const loanRequest = action.payload;

  return Object.freeze({
    ...loanRequest
  });
```

```
}

export default handleActions({
    [actions.submitLoanRequest]: submitLoanRequest
  },
  initialState
);
```

Selectors

The total interest is a computed value. We are not going to save it as state, but compute it every time the user presses the submit button. For this, we are going to use the computeLoan() selector function.

```
function computeLoan(loanRequest){
  const amount = Number.parseInt(loanRequest.amount);
  const term = Number.parseInt(loanRequest.term);
  const interest = Number.parseInt(loanRequest.interest);
  const totalInterest = amount * term * interest / 100;
  const totalPaid = amount + totalInterest;

  return {
    totalInterest,
    totalPaid
  };
}

export { computeLoan };
```

Testing the Selector

Here is a simple test of the computeLoan() selector.

```
import { computeLoan } from './selectors';

test('computeLoan', function(){
  const amount = 10000;
  const term = 5;
  const interest = 5
  const expectOutput = {
    totalInterest: 2500,
    totalPaid: 12500
```

```
  };

  expect(computeLoan({amount, term, interest}))
    .toEqual(expectOutput);
});
```

Connecting

The `LoanForm` view reads the `loanRequest` object from the store and dispatches the `submitLoanRequest` action.

```
import { connect } from 'react-redux';
import { submitLoanRequest } from './actions';

function mapState(loanRequest){
  return {
    loanRequest
  }
}

export default connect(
  mapState,
  { submitLoanRequest }
)(LoanForm);
```

The loan information is computed from state using the `computeLoan()` selector and then is displayed in the `LoanResult` view.

```
import { connect } from 'react-redux';
import { computeLoan } from './selectors';

function mapState(state){
  return {
    loan: computeLoan(state)
  }
}

export default connect(
  mapState
)(LoanResult);
```

Root View

The `App` view uses the `LoanForm` and `LoanResult` views to generate the interface.

```
import React from 'react';
import LoanForm from './LoanForm';
import LoanResult from './LoanResult';

function App() {
  return (
    <div>
      <LoanForm />
      <LoanResult />
    </div>
  );
}

export default App;
```

Final Thoughts

Uncontrolled inputs do not have the value or the `onChange` callback defined.

We can read the values of uncontrolled inputs on the `onSubmit` event with the help of the `FormData` object.

HTML5 validation attributes can be used for form validation.

`pipe()` creates a pipeline of functions where the output of one function is the input for the next one.

Chapter 10: Loan Calculator App with Controlled Inputs

Next, we are going to implement the `LoanForm` view with controlled inputs.

Controlled inputs have both the value and the `onChange` event set.

State

This time, we need two properties for storing the loan request object.

The `loanRequestInput` stores the current loan request that can be changed without triggering a loan computation.

The `loanRequest` stores the loan request for which the computation was triggered.

```
const initialLoanRequest = Object.freeze({
  amount: 10000,
  term: 5,
  interest: 5
});

const initialState = Object.freeze({
  loanRequestInput: initialLoanRequest,
  loanRequest: initialLoanRequest
});
```

Actions

In order to change the state when the user types into the input fields, we need a new action, `changeLoanRequest`.

```
const changeLoanRequest = createAction('CHANGE_LOAN_REQUEST');

export { changeLoanRequest };
```

View Functions

All inputs, in the `LoanForm` view function must have both the value and the `onChange` properties set.

```
import React from 'react';
import pipe from 'lodash/flow';
import { partial } from 'lodash';
import { preventDefault } from './helpers';

function LoanForm({
    loanRequest,
    changeLoanRequest,
    submitLoanRequest }){

  function handleChange(e){
    const change = Object.freeze({
      name: e.target.name,
      value: e.target.value
    });

    changeLoanRequest(change);
  }

  const handleSubmit = partial(submitLoanRequest, loanRequest)

  return(
    <form onSubmit={pipe(preventDefault, handleSubmit)}>
    <div>
     <label htmlFor="amount">Loan amount</label>
     <input
       name="amount"
       type="number"
```

```
        value={loanRequest.amount}
        onChange={handleChange}
        required
       />
    </div>
    <div>
     <label htmlFor="term">Loan term in years</label>
     <input
       name="term"
       type="number"
       value={loanRequest.term}
       onChange={handleChange}
       required
      />
    </div>
    <div>
      <label htmlFor="interest">Interest rate per year</label>
     <input
       name="interest"
       type="number"
       value={loanRequest.interest}
       onChange={handleChange}
       required
      />
    </div>
    <div>
      <button type="submit">
        Calculate
      </button>
    </div>
    </form>
  )
}
```

handleChange(e) creates a name-value pair object from the input change event and calls the changeLoanRequest() callback with it.

handleSubmit() calls the submitLoanRequest() callback with the loanRequest object.

Input Change Helpers

We can create a helper function to extract the change from the input change event as an object with the `name` and `value` properties.

```
import pipe from 'lodash/flow';

function getInputChange(e){
  return Object.freeze({
    name: e.target.name,
    value: e.target.value
  });
}

function withChange(callback){
  return pipe(
    getInputChange,
    callback
  )
}

export { getInputChange, withChange };
```

The `getInputChange(e)` extracts the `name-value` pair from the input change event.

`withChange(callback)` takes a callback function and returns a new function expecting the input change event. It uses `getInputChange()` to compute the `name-value` pair object and then uses it to call the original callback.

```
const handleChange = withChange(changeLoanRequest);
```

Connecting

The connected `LoanForm` view reads the current `loanRequest` from the `loanRequestInput` state branch and dispatches both the `submitLoanRequest` and `changeLoanRequest` actions.

```
import { connect } from 'react-redux';
import { submitLoanRequest, changeLoanRequest } from './actions'

function mapState({ loanRequestInput }){
  return {
```

```
    loanRequest: loanRequestInput
  }
}

export default connect(
  mapState,
  { submitLoanRequest, changeLoanRequest }
)(LoanForm);
```

Update Functions

The update function needs to handle two actions.

On the changeLoanRequest action, the loanRequestInput changes. The changeLoanRequest() function dynamically changes just one property of the loanRequestInput state branch.

On the submitLoanRequest action, the loanRequest state branch changes.

```
import { handleActions } from 'redux-actions';
import * as actions from './actions';

//updaters
function changeLoanRequest(state, action){
  const input = action.payload;
  const loanRequestInput = {
    ...state.loanRequestInput,
    [input.name]: input.value
  };

  return Object.freeze({
    ...state,
    loanRequestInput
  });
}

function submitLoanRequest(state, action){
  const loanRequest = action.payload;

  return Object.freeze({
    ...state,
```

```
        loanRequest
    });
}

export default handleActions({
    [actions.changeLoanRequest]: changeLoanRequest,
    [actions.submitLoanRequest]: submitLoanRequest
  },
  initialState
);
```

Final Thoughts

Controlled inputs have both the value and the **onChange** attributes set.

Helpers can be used to extract the **name-value** pair from the input change event and create a new callback with the **name-value** pair already applied.

Working with controlled inputs requires to have an associated state.

Chapter 11: Toast Notification Module

A toast message is a short message that is displayed on the top or bottom of the screen and disappears after a few seconds. It is usually used as feedback after an action.

The Toast Notification module allows sending toast messages.

Let's start building it.

State

The state is represented by an array of toast notifications.

```
const initialState = [];
```

Actions

We will need two actions, one for adding a toast to the list, and another one for deleting a toast.

```
import { createAction } from 'redux-actions';

const addToast = createAction('ADD_TOAST');
const deleteToast = createAction('DELETE_TOAST');

export { addToast, deleteToast };
```

View Functions

The `ToastList` view function takes a list of toasts and transforms it into a visual interface.

We can start by creating the `ToastItem` view function for the visual representation of a single item on the list.

```
import React from 'react';
import { partial } from 'lodash';

function ToastItem({toast, deleteToast}){
  return (
    <div>
      <div>{toast.message}</div>
      <div>
        <button
          type="button"
          onClick={partial(deleteToast, toast)}>
            X
        </button>
      </div>
    </div>
  )
}

export default ToastItem;
```

The `ToastList` transforms a list of toasts objects into a list of `ToastItem` elements.

```
import React from 'react';
import ToastItem from './ToastItem';

function ToastList({toasts, deleteToast}){
  return (
    <div>
      { toasts.map(toast =>
          <ToastItem
            key={toast.id}
            toast={toast}
            deleteToast={deleteToast} /> )
      }
    </div>
  )
}
```

Connecting

The `ToastList` view reads the toasts to display and dispatches the `deleteToast` action.

```
import { connect } from 'react-redux';
import { deleteToast } from './actions';

function mapState(state){
  const { toasts } = state;
  return {
    toasts
  }
}

export default connect(
  mapState,
  { deleteToast }
)(ToastList)
```

Note that the `ToastList` view is connected and the `ListItem` view is not. This approach requires to set the `deleteToast()` callback from the `ToastList` view for each `ListItem` element. The alternative is to connect the `ListItem` view and map the `deleteToast()` callback to the `deleteToast()` action creator. This way the `ListItem` view connects directly to the store and not via its parent.

Here is how the `ListItem` view can connect to the store and dispatch the `deleteToast` action.

```
import { connect } from 'react-redux';
import { deleteToast } from './actions';

export default connect(
    null,
    { deleteToast }
)(ToastItem);
```

In this case, the `ToastList` view just reads the list of toasts from the store.

```
import { connect } from 'react-redux';

function mapState(state){
```

```
        const { toasts } = state;
        return {
            toasts
        }
}

export default connect(mapState)(ToastList);
```

Update Functions

We need to handle the two actions.

`addToast()` takes the current toast list and creates a new toast list with the input toast added.

`deleteToast()` takes the current toast list and creates a new toast list with the input toast deleted.

```
import { handleActions } from 'redux-actions';
import * as actions from './actions';

function addToast(toasts, action){
  const toast = action.payload;
  return [...toasts, toast];
}

function deleteToast(toasts, action){
  const toastId = action.payload.id;
  const newToasts = toasts.filter(({id})=> id !== toastId);
  return newToasts;
}

export default handleActions({
    [actions.addToast]: addToast,
    [actions.deleteToast]: deleteToast
  },
  initialState
);
```

Both update functions are pure. They don't modify the input `toasts` array but create a new one.

Testing the Update Functions

Tests can be written for adding and deleting a toast.

```
import reducer from './reducer';
import * as actions from './actions';

test('addToast', function(){
  const toasts = [
    {id:1, message: 'First toast'}
  ];
  const action =
    actions.addToast({id:2, message: 'Second toast'});
  const expectOutput = [
    {id:1, message: 'First toast'},
    {id:2, message: 'Second toast'}
  ];
  expect(reducer(toasts, action)).toEqual(expectOutput);
});

test('deleteToast', function(){
  const toasts = [
    {id:1, message: 'First toast'},
    {id:2, message: 'Second toast'}
  ];
  const action =
    actions.deleteToast({id:2, message: 'Second toast'});
  const expectOutput = [
    {id:1, message: 'First toast'}
  ];
  expect(reducer(toasts, action)).toEqual(expectOutput);
});
```

Asynchronous Actions

There are situations when we want to do asynchronous tasks like sending timer events or doing network requests. Both these tasks are impure and cannot be executed inside the pure update functions.

Redux Thunk is a middleware for Redux that allows writing a new kind of action creators that return a function instead of an action. The returned function is called a thunk.

With Redux Thunk we can dispatch plain objects and functions as actions. Dispatching plain objects modifies the state. Dispatching functions executes the logic inside the functions and then dispatches other actions.

Thunk functions define operations that can do asynchronous tasks and dispatch several actions. These functions are called operations or just thunks.

Operations can be a place for encapsulating impure code. It can also be a place for coordinating multiple state updates.

The thunk function receives the store methods `dispatch()` and `getState()` as parameters.

Let's implement a thunk action that creates a toast and removes it after a few seconds.

```
import * as actions from './actions';
import uuid from 'uuid';

function addToast(message){
  return function(dispatch){
    const id = uuid();

    const toast = {
      id,
      message
    }

    dispatch(actions.addToast(toast));
    setTimeout(function(){
      dispatch(actions.deleteToast(toast));
    }, 5000);
  }
}

export { addToast };
```

The `addToast()` is an asynchronous action creator creating a thunk. The thunk function generates a unique id and then dispatches the `addToast` action. After a few seconds it dispatches the `deleteToast` action.

The unique identifier is generated using a utility function from the uuid library. The `uuid()` function is impure as it is not a deterministic function.

Module

The Toast Notification should be a separate module. The module will be in a separate folder with its own update function.

The `toastsReducer()` update function manages just the toast notification part of the application state.

Root Update Function

The Redux store needs a single update function as input. This is called the root reducer.

The `combineReducers()` helper function can combine several update functions managing parts of the state into one root update function.

```
import { combineReducers } from 'redux';
import toastsReducer from './toasts/reducer';

export default combineReducers({
  toasts: toastsReducer
});
```

Other Views

We can create a new view function outside the notification module that can dispatch `addToast` thunk actions.

```
import React from "react";
import { connect } from "react-redux";
import { partial } from "lodash";

import { addToast } from "./toasts/operations";

function AddToast({ addToast }){
  return (
    <div>
      <button
      type="button"
      onClick={partial(addToast, "A new toast message")}>
        ADD TOAST
      </button>
    </div>
```

```
    )
}

export default connect(
  null,
  { addToast }
)(AddToast)
```

Root View

The `App` root view renders the screen using the `AddToast` and `ToastList` views.

```
import React from "react";
import AddToast from "./AddToast";
import ToastList from "./toasts/ToastList";

function App() {
  return (
    <div>
      <AddToast />
      <ToastList />
    </div>
  );
}

export default App;
```

Entry Point

In the application entry point, we are going to use the root update function to initialize the store. For an easier integration of Redux DevTools we will to use the redux-devtools-extension package.

```
npm install redux-devtools-extension --save
```

The store is created using the root update function and the thunk middleware together with the Redux DevTools activated.

```
import { createStore, applyMiddleware } from 'redux';
import { composeWithDevTools } from 'redux-devtools-extension';
import thunk from 'redux-thunk';
import rootReducer from "./rootReducer";
```

```
const store = createStore(rootReducer, composeWithDevTools(
  applyMiddleware(thunk)
));
```

Final Thoughts

The `redux-thunk` middleware allows writing asynchronous action creators that return functions instead of plain objects.

Update functions are pure functions and do not contain asynchronous logic.

Thunk actions can encapsulate asynchronous calls and other impure code.

Chapter 12: Weather App

The Weather App uses the OpenWeatherMap.org API to show the weather in a city. The application allows adding the city weather to a list showing the weather in different cities.

State

The initial state is made of an empty text used for searching a city by name and an empty list of cities.

```
const initialState = Object.freeze({
  cityName = '',
  cities = []
});
```

Actions

We need two actions. One for changing the `cityName` based on the user input, and another for adding the city to the list.

```
import { createAction } from 'redux-actions';

const changeCityName = createAction('CHANGE_CITY_NAME');
const addCity = createAction('ADD_CITY');

export { changeCityName, addCity };
```

Update Functions

All the state can be managed with one update function, but I think it is a better idea to split state management between two update functions in this case. It is a good idea in general, to split the state management between update functions as the application grows more complex.

listReducer()

The `listReducer()` update function manages the array of cities. When the `addCity` action is dispatched it adds a new city to the list.

```
import { handleActions } from 'redux-actions';
import * as actions from '../actions';

const initialState = [];

//updaters
function addCity(cities, action){
  const city = action.payload;
  if(!isCityInList(cities, city)){
    return [...cities, city];
  }
  return cities;
}

function isCityInList(cities, newCity){
  const existingCity = cities.find(city=>city.id === newCity.id);
  return existingCity != null;
}

export default handleActions({
    [actions.addCity]: addCity
  },
  initialState
);
```

Testing listReducer()

For verifying the `listReducer()`, we can create a test adding a new city to the list.

```
import listReducer from './listReducer';
import * as actions from '../actions';

test('addCity add city', function(){
```

```
  const cities = []
  const action = actions.addCity('Malaga');
  const expectOutput = [
    'Malaga'
  ];
  expect(listReducer(cities, action)).toEqual(expectOutput);
});
```

Another test can check the addition of an existing city to the list.

```
test('addCity does not add existing city', function(){
  const cities = [
    'Sorrento'
  ]
  const action = actions.addCity('Sorrento');
  const expectOutput = [
    'Sorrento'
  ];
  expect(listReducer(cities, action)).toEqual(expectOutput);
});
```

searchReducer()

The `searchReducer()` update function manages the `cityName` state branch. It changes the state on the `changeCityName` action and clears the state on the `addCity` action.

```
import { handleActions } from 'redux-actions';
import * as actions from '../actions';

const initialState = '';

//updaters
function changeCityName(name, action){
  return action.payload.value;
}

function clearCityName(name, action){
  return '';
}

export default handleActions({
```

```
    [actions.changeCityName]: changeCityName,
    [actions.addCity]: clearCityName
  },
  initialState
);
```

Root Update Function

The `combineReducers()` helper can combine the two update functions into one root update function that can be passed to the `createStore()` utility.

```
import { combineReducers } from "redux";
import listReducer from "./reducers/listReducer";
import searchReducer from "./reducers/searchReducer";

export default combineReducers({
  cities: listReducer,
  cityName: searchReducer
})
```

API Utils

The API utils are functions that encapsulate the network requests. They are impure.

In order to use the OpenWeatherMap.org, an API key (APPID) is needed.

We are going to use the axios library for making network requests.

`npm install --save axios`

The axios library improves the way we are doing network requests.

```
import axios from 'axios';

const apiKey = '00000000000000000000000000000000';
const baseUrl = 'http://api.openweathermap.org/data/2.5';

function fetchCityWeather(cityName){
  const url = `${baseUrl}/weather?q=${cityName}&APPID=${apiKey}`;
  return axios.get(url);
}
```

```
export { fetchCityWeather };
```

The network calls return promises.

Promises

A promise is a reference to a future result of an asynchronous operation.

Asynchronous operations do not block the application while waiting for the result. The network call is an asynchronous operation, it does not block the application while waiting for the result from the server.

Asynchronous operations start the task and return immediately. The operation may finish somewhere in the future.

A promise can be in one of the three statuses: pending, resolved or rejected.

A promise is actually an object with two important methods `then()` and `catch()` that can be chained.

`then()` can be used to append a success handler to the promise. It returns a new promise.

`catch()` appends a rejection handler to the promise, and returns a new promise. If there is an error at any step, the chain control jumps to the closest rejection handler down the chain.

Operations

The `fetchCity()` operation coordinates the task of getting the city weather and adding it to the list.

```
import * as actions from './actions';
import { fetchCityWeather } from './api';

function fetchCity(cityName){
  return function(dispatch){
    fetchCityWeather(cityName)
      .then(selectTemperature)
      .then(actions.addCity)
      .then(dispatch)
  }
}
```

```
function selectTemperature(response){
  const { id, name } = response.data;
  const { temp } =  response.data.main;
  return {
    id,
    name,
    temp
  }
}

export { fetchCity };
```

Promises support a chaining system that allows passing data through a set of functions. The result of `fetchCityWeather()` is passed as input to `selectTemperature()`. The result is then passed as input to the `addCity()` action creator that builds an action. The action object is then passed to the `dispatch()` function.

View Functions

The `CityList` view maps the `cities` array to a visual interface. We can start by extracting out the creation of the UI for a single list item into its own view function.

```
import React from 'react';

function CityItem({city}){
  return (
    <div>
      <div>{city.name}</div>
      <div>{city.temp}</div>
    </div>
  )
}

export default CityItem;
```

Then we can use the `CityItem` view inside the `CityList` view.

```
import React from 'react';
import CityItem from './CityItem';

function CityList({cities}){
```

```
    return (
      <div>
       { cities.map(city =>
           <CityItem
             key={city.id}
             city={city} /> )
       }
      </div>
    )
}
```

The `CitySearch` view function allows adding a city to the list. It dispatches the `fetchCity` operation when pressing the Add City button.

```
import React from 'react';
import { partial } from 'lodash';
import { withChange } from './helpers';

function CitySearch({ cityName, changeCityName, fetchCity }){
  return(
    <div>
     <input
       type="text"
       value={cityName}
       onChange={withChange(changeCityName)} />

     <button
       type="button"
       onClick={partial(fetchCity, cityName)} >
        Add City
     </button>
    </div>
  )
}
```

Connecting

The connected `CityList` view reads the `cities` array from the store.

```
import { connect } from 'react-redux';

function mapState({cities}){
```

```
        return {
            cities
        }
}
```

```
export default connect(
    mapState
)(CityList)
```

The connected `CitySearch` view reads the `cityName` from the store and dispatches the `changeCityName` action and the `fetchCity` operation.

```
import { connect } from 'react-redux';
import { changeCityName } from './actions';
import { fetchCity } from './operations';

function mapState({cityName}){
  return {
    cityName
  }
}

export default connect(
  mapState,
  { changeCityName, fetchCity }
)(CitySearch)
```

Root View

The root view, `App`, renders the screen using the `CitySearch` and `CityList` views.

```
import React from 'react';
import CitySearch from './cityWeather/CitySearch';
import CityList from './cityWeather/CityList';

function App() {
  return (
    <div>
      <CitySearch />
      <CityList />
    </div>
```

```
    );
}

export default App;
```

Final Thoughts

State management can be split between smaller update functions managing parts of that state. `combineReducers()` can then be used to combine smaller update function into the root update function.

The API util functions encapsulate network requests. Network requests return promises.

Promises are references to future results of asynchronous operations.

Chapter 13: Hacker News App

The Hacker News App uses the public API to get the most popular posts and displays them. The application shows the top posts and allows to retrieve more of them.

State

The state, in this case, is in relation to the way the data is got from the Hacker News API.

`storiesIds` keeps all the story ids go from the API.

`topStories` contains the top stories with full details.

```
const initialState = Object.freeze({
  storiesIds: [],
  topStories: []
});
```

Actions

We will need two actions: the `setStoriesIds` action for storing all the ids retrieved from the API, and the `addTopStories` action for adding more detailed stories when the user clicks the Show More button.

```
import { createAction } from 'redux-actions';

const setStoriesIds = createAction('SET_STORIES_IDS');
const addTopStories = createAction('ADD_TOP_STORIES');

export {
```

```
  setStoriesIds,
  addTopStories
};
```

Update Functions

On the `setStoriesIds` action, the state is updated with the new ids.

On the `addTopStories` action, the new detailed stories are added to the existing ones.

```
import { handleActions } from 'redux-actions';
import * as actions from './actions';

//updaters
function setStoriesIds(state, action){
  const storiesIds = action.payload;
  return {
    ...state,
    storiesIds
  }
}

function addTopStories(state, action){
  const newStories = action.payload;
  const topStories = state.topStories.concat(newStories);
  return {
    ...state,
    topStories
  };
}

export default handleActions({
    [actions.setStoriesIds]: setStoriesIds,
    [actions.addTopStories]: addTopStories
  },
  initialState
);
```

Selectors

We can create a selector for retrieving the total number of detailed stories.

```
function getTopStoriesNumber(state){
  return state.topStories.length;
}

export { getTopStoriesNumber };
```

API Utils

There will be two fetch functions, `fetchTopStoriesIds()` for getting all the stories ids and `fetchStory()` for getting the details of one story.

```
import axios from 'axios';

const baseUrl = 'https://hacker-news.firebaseio.com/v0';

function fetchTopStoriesIds(){
  const url = `${baseUrl}/topstories.json`;
  return axios.get(url).then(getData);
}

function fetchStory(id){
  const url = `${baseUrl}/item/${id}.json`;
  return axios.get(url).then(getData);
}

function getData(request){
  return request.data;
}

export default { fetchTopStoriesIds, fetchStory };
```

Operations

Before defining the operations we need a helper function. The `fetchDetailsForStories()` utility function takes a list of ids and returns a promise containing the details for all of them.

```
import api from "./api";

function fetchDetailsForStories(ids){
  const promises = ids.map(api.fetchStory);
  return Promise.all(promises);
```

}

`api.fetchStory()` takes an id and returns a promise containing the detailed story with that id. `ids.map(api.fetchStory)` converts the list of ids into a list o promises.

`Promise.all()` returns a new promise that resolves when all promises have resolved, or rejects when one of the promises rejects. This means that the `fetchDetailsForStories()` returns a promise that either succeeds and has the details for all stories or fails.

The detailed stories are retrieved in batches of N stories.
The `showMoreStories()` operation gets the details for the next N stories

```
import * as actions from './actions';
import { getTopStoriesNumber } from './selectors';

const maxNoOfNewStories = 10;

function showMoreStories(){
  return function(dispatch, getState){
    const state = getState();
    const { storiesIds } = state;

    const from = getTopStoriesNumber(state);
    const to = from + maxNoOfNewStories;
    const newIds = storiesIds.slice(from, to);

    fetchDetailsForStories(newIds)
      .then(actions.addTopStories)
      .then(dispatch);
  }
}
```

It first gets all the stories ids and the number of stories that already have details from the current state. It extracts from the list with all the ids the next N ids for which details should be retrieved from the backend. Then it uses the previous utility function `fetchDetailsForStories()` to take the details for all those ids.

The promise chaining creates a pipeline. The stories retrieved by `fetchDetailsForStories()` are passed to the `actions.addTopStories()` action creator that builds an action. The action object is then given to the `dispatch()` function.

The `fetchTopStories()` operation gets all the ids and the details for the first N stories

```
function fetchTopStories(){
  return function(dispatch){
    api.fetchTopStoriesIds()
      .then(actions.setStoriesIds)
      .then(dispatch)
      .then(showMoreStories)
      .then(dispatch)
  }
}
```

```
export { fetchTopStories, showMoreStories };
```

Again, the promise chaining creates a pipeline. The ids get by `fetchTopStoriesIds` are passed as input to `actions.setStoriesIds` action creator that builds a new action. The newly created action is then dispatched. Next the `showMoreStories` operation is created and dispatched.

Note that `fetchTopStories` operation dispatches another operation, `showMoreStories`.

View Functions

The `TopStories` view function takes a list of stories and creates the UI for them.

We can extract the UI for a single story into the `StoryItem` view function.

```
import React from 'react';

function StoryItem({ story }){
  return (
    <div>
      <div>{story.title}</div>
    </div>
  )
}

export default StoryItem
```

Next, the `TopStories` view uses the `StoryItem` view to create the UI for the list of stories.

```
import React from 'react';
import StoryItem from './StoryItem';

function TopStories({ stories, showMoreStories }){
  return (
    <div>
     <div>
       { stories.map(story =>
           <StoryItem
             key={story.id}
             story={story} /> )
       }
     </div>
    <div>
      <button
        onClick={showMoreStories}
        type="button">
         Show More
      </button>
    </div>
   </div>
  )
}
```

Connecting

The `TopStories` view reads the `topStories` state branch from the store and dispatches the `showMoreStories` operation.

```
import { connect } from 'react-redux';
import { showMoreStories } from './operations';

function mapState({topStories}){
  return {
    stories: topStories
  }
}

export default connect(
```

```
  mapState,
  { showMoreStories }
)(TopStories);
```

Root View

The `App` root view uses the `TopStories` view function to create the page UI.

```
import React from 'react';
import TopStories from './TopStories';

function App() {
  return (
    <div>
      <TopStories />
    </div>
  );
}

export default App;
```

Entry Point

In the application entry point, the `fetchTopStories` operation is dispatched.

```
import {fetchTopStories} from './operations';

store.dispatch(fetchTopStories())
```

Final Thoughts

Operations become the place for the orchestration logic coordinating the store updates.

Operations dispatch plain actions, but they can also dispatch other operations.

Chapter 14: Show More Component

Let's build a simple Show More component. It takes as input a title and a content. Initially, only the title is shown. When the Show More button is pressed the content is displayed.

State

The state for this component is just a boolean deciding if the content is shown or not.

```
const initialState = false;
```

Actions

We need one action for toggling the display of the content.

```
import { createAction } from 'redux-actions';

const toggleShowMore = createAction('TOGGLE_SHOW_MORE');

export { toggleShowMore };
```

View Function

The view function takes the `title` and the content as props. The content is passed using the `children` property.

```
import React from 'react';
import { toggleShowMore } from './actions';

function ShowMore({showMore, toggleShowMore, title, children}){
```

```
    return (
      <div>
        <h2>{ title }</h2>
        <div>
          <button
            onClick={toggleShowMore}
            type="button">
              ShowMore
          </button>
        </div>
        <div>
         { showMore ? children : "" }
        </div>
      </div>
    )
}
```

Connecting

The `showMore` property deciding if the content should be shown or not is read from the store.

The `toggleShowMore()` callback dispatches the `toggleShowMore` action.

```
import { connect } from 'react-redux';

function mapState({ showMore }) {
  return {
    showMore
  }
}

export default connect(
  mapState,
  { toggleShowMore }
)(ShowMore);
```

Update Function

The update function toggles the boolean value.

```
import { handleActions } from 'redux-actions';
```

```
import * as actions from './actions';

function toggleShowMore(showMore, action){
  return !showMore;
}

const reducer = handleActions({
  [actions.toggleShowMore]: toggleShowMore
}, initialState);

export default reducer;
```

Root Update Function

The `ShowMore` component has its own state branch, `showMore`, managed by the `showMoreReducer()` update function.

```
import { combineReducers } from 'redux';
import showMoreReducer from './ShowMore/reducer';

export default combineReducers({
  showMore: showMoreReducer
});
```

Root View

The App root view uses the `ShowMore` view to display several panels with their own title and content.

```
import React from 'react';
import ShowMore from './ShowMore/ShowMore'

function App() {
  return (
    <div>
      <ShowMore title="Title1">
        This is my content1
      </ShowMore>
      <ShowMore title="Title2">
        This is my content2
      </ShowMore>
      <ShowMore title="Title3">
```

```
      This is my content3
    </ShowMore>
  </div>
);
}
```

`export default App;`

At this point, we notice a problem. When the content of one of the `ShowMore` components is opened all the other components are opened.

Reusing the Update Function

We need a way to declare each view with its own UI state. We can, of course, create a state branch for each view, but the existing update function cannot make a difference between them.

```
export default combineReducers({
  showMore: combineReducers({
    show1: showMoreReducer,
    show2: showMoreReducer,
    show3: showMoreReducer
  })
});
```

In order to differentiate between actions from different `ShowMore` views, the action itself should have a new meta property like `name`. Also when reading the information from the state we need again the `name` to select the proper state branch.

```
import { connect } from 'react-redux';

function mapState({ showMore }, {name}) {
  return {
    showMore: showMore[name]
  }
}

function mapDispatch(dispatch, {name}){
  return {
    toggleShowMore(){
      let action = toggleShowMore();
      action.meta = { name };
```

```
      dispatch(action)
    }
  }
}

export default connect(
  mapState,
  mapDispatch
)(ShowMore);
```

The logic for creating an action with the **name** meta property can be encapsulated inside a helper like **nameAction()**.

```
import { nameAction } from '../helpers';

function mapDispatch(dispatch, {name}){
  return {
    toggleShowMore(){
      const createAction = nameAction(toggleShowMore, name);
      dispatch(createAction())
    }
  }
}
```

We can also create a helper function like **nameActions()** taking a list of action creators and returning a new list of action creators that set the **name** meta property when creating the plain action object.

```
import { connect } from 'react-redux';
import { nameActions } from '../helpers';

export default connect(
  mapState,
  nameActions({toggleShowMore})
)(ShowMore);
```

In the **App** root view, the **name** property should be set on each instance of the **ShowMore** view.

```
import React from 'react';
import ShowMore from './ShowMore/ShowMore'

function App() {
```

```
    return (
      <div>
        <ShowMore title="Title1" name="show1" >
          This is my content1
        </ShowMore>
        <ShowMore title="Title2" name="show2">
          This is my content2
        </ShowMore>
        <ShowMore title="Title3" name="show3">
          This is my content3
        </ShowMore>
      </div>
    );
}

export default App;
```

The update function managing the state branch for a specific ShowMore view should only handle the actions containing the specific name meta information. This can be done with a new helper, nameReducer().

```
import { combineReducers } from 'redux';
import showMoreReducer from './ShowMore/reducer';
import { nameReducer } from './helpers';

export default combineReducers({
  showMore: combineReducers({
    show1: nameReducer(showMoreReducer, 'show1'),
    show2: nameReducer(showMoreReducer, 'show2'),
    show3: nameReducer(showMoreReducer, 'show3')
  })
});
```

Helpers

Below is the implementation of the previous helpers.

nameReducer(reducer, name) takes an update function and returns a new update function handling only the actions with a specific name meta information.

```
function nameReducer(reducer, reducerName) {
  return function newReducer(state, action){
```

```
    let name;
    if(action && action.meta){
      name = action.meta.name
    }
    const isInitialization = state === undefined
    if (name !== reducerName && !isInitialization) return state

    return reducer(state, action);
  }
}
```

nameAction(actionCreator, name) takes an action creator and a name, and returns a new action creator creating the same action, but with the name set as meta information.

```
function nameAction(actionCreator, name){
  return function newActionCreator(){
    let actionDto = actionCreator();
    actionDto.meta = { name };
    return actionDto;
  }
}
```

nameActions(map) takes a map of action creators and creates a new map of action creators that builds actions with the name set as meta information. The name is read from the view properties.

```
import { bindActionCreators } from 'redux';

function nameActions(actionCreatorsMap){
  return function mapDispatchToProps(dispatch, {name}) {
    const map = {};
    Object.keys(actionCreatorsMap).forEach(actionName => {
      const actionCreator = actionCreatorsMap[actionName];
      map[actionName] = nameAction(actionCreator, name);
    });
    return bindActionCreators(map, dispatch)
  }
}
```

View Function with Local State

In this case, a simpler solution is to create a view with local state.

The useState() hook, part of the React Hooks API, allows defining a view function component with local state.

```
import React, { useState } from 'react';

const initialState = false;

function toggleShowMore(showMore){
  return !showMore;
}

function ShowMore({ title, children }){
  const [showMore, setShowMore] = useState(initialState);

  function onToggleShowMore(){
    setShowMore(toggleShowMore);
  }

  return (
    <div>
      <h2>{ title }</h2>
      <div>
        <button
          onClick={onToggleShowMore}
          type="button">
          ShowMore
        </button>
      </div>
      <div>
        { showMore ? children : "" }
      </div>
    </div>
  )
}

export default ShowMore;
```

useState() returns the current state and a function to update it.

The **showMore** variable hols the current state. It can be used only in a read-only way.

The `setShowMore()` function updates the state stored in the `showMore` variable and re-renders the `ShowMore` view with the new value. `setShowMore()` can be invoked with the new value, or it can be invoked with a pure update function like `toggleShowMore()` returning the new value. The pure update function takes the current state and returns the new state.

The view function is no longer a pure function as it has local state.

Final Thoughts

Reusing a view with the UI state in the store requires a state branch for each instance. Additional meta information like the `name` property is required to differentiate between different instances of the same view.

The `useState()` hook can define local state into view functions.

View functions with local state can be a better alternative for creating reusable views with their own UI state.

Chapter 15: NYT App

The NYT App connects to the New York Times API and displays the best-selling books, movie reviews, and the most popular articles. The application contains several view pages. The main page allows access to the other pages.

Books

Let's start with the books view page.

State

We are going to store all the book categories and the best selling books in the selected category. The `bestBooks` branch stores the list of books and the category-name of those books.

```
const initialState = Object.freeze({
  categories : [],
  bestBooks : { categoryName: '', list: [] }
});
```

Actions

Two actions are needed, one for updating the book categories and another one for updating the best selling books in the selected category.

```
import { createAction } from 'redux-actions';

const setBookCategories = createAction('SET_BOOK_CATEGORIES');
const setBooks = createAction('SET_BOOKS');

export {
```

```
  setBookCategories,
  setBooks
}
```

View Functions

We are going to build views for displaying the list of categories and the list of books.

This time the categories view and the books view are going to be separate pages. We are going to use the React Router library to define the routes to these pages and create the links pointing to them.

Let's start building the views.

As already said, it is a good practice to separate the UI for a single item into its own view function. The `CategoryItem` view renders a single category.

```
import React from 'react';
import { Link } from 'react-router-dom';

function CategoryItem({category}){
  return (
   <div>
     <Link
       to={`/books/${category.id}/`}>
         {category.name}
     </Link>
   </div>
  )
}
```

```
export default CategoryItem;
```

The `<Link>` component allows to navigate to different routes defined in the application. It can be imagined like an anchor link. Navigation links created with `<Link>` do not result in a page refresh. To navigate to a route, we specify the pathname in the `to` property.

The `Categories` view renders a list of categories.

```
import React from 'react';
import { Link } from 'react-router-dom';
```

```
import CategoryItem from './CategoryItem';

function Categories({categories}){
  return (
    <div>
      <div><Link to="/">Home</Link></div>
      <h2>Categories</h2>
      <div>
        { categories.map(category =>
            <CategoryItem
              category={category}
              key={category.id} /> )
        }
      </div>
    </div>
  )
}
```

BookItem renders a single item on the list.

```
import React from 'react';

function BookItem({book}){
  return (
    <div >
      <div>{book.title}</div>
      <div>{book.author}</div>
    </div>
  )
}

export default BookItem;
```

The BookList view function renders a list of books.

```
import React from 'react';
import BookItem from './BookItem'

function BookList({ books }){
  return (
    <div>
      <h2>{books.list_name}</h2>
```

```
      <div>
        { books.books.map(book =>
            <BookItem
              book={book}
              key={book.id} /> )
        }
      </div>
    </div>
  )
}
```

Update Functions

When the `setBookCategories` action is dispatched, the `categories` state branch is updated.

When the `setBooks` action is dispatched, the `bestBooks` state branch is updated.

```
import { handleActions } from 'redux-actions';
import * as actions from "./actions";

//updaters
function setBooks(state, action){
  const bestBooks = action.payload;
  return {
    ...state,
    bestBooks
  }
}

function setBookCategories(state, action){
  const categories = action.payload;
  return {
    ...state,
    categories
  };
}

export default handleActions({
    [actions.setBooks]: setBooks,
    [actions.setBookCategories]: setBookCategories
```

```
  },
  initialState
);
```

Connecting

We are going to set the books management in a modular way with its own **books** branch. In this case, when connecting to the store we need to extract the **books** branch first.

The connected **Categories** view reads the **categories** from the store.

```
import { connect } from 'react-redux';

function mapState({books}){
  return {
    categories: books.categories
  }
}

export default connect(mapState)(Categories);
```

The connected **BookList** view reads the **bestBooks** from the store.

```
import { connect } from 'react-redux';

function mapState({books}){
  return {
    books: books.bestBooks
  }
}

export default connect(mapState)(BookList);
```

API Utils

In order to access the NYT API, we need to create an account and get the API key.

We are going to define two API functions for getting the book categories and the best selling books.

```
import axios from 'axios';
```

```
const apiKey = '00000000000000000000000000000000';
const baseUrl = 'https://api.nytimes.com/svc/books/v3/lists';

function getResults(response){
  return (response && response.data)
    ? response.data.results
    : response;
}

function fetchBookCategories(){
  const url = `${baseUrl}/names.json?api-key=${apiKey}`;
  return axios(url)
    .then(getResults);
}

function fetchBooks(category){
  const url =
    `${baseUrl}/current/${category}.json?api-key=${apiKey}`;
  return axios(url)
    .then(getResults)
}

export default {
  fetchBookCategories,
  fetchBooks
};
```

Operations

Operations fetch data from the NYT API and update the state.

`fetchBookCategories` retrives all the book categories and then creates and dispatches the `setBookCategories` action to update the state with those categories.

```
import api from "./api";
import * as actions from './actions';

function fetchBookCategories(){
  return function(dispatch){
    return api.fetchBookCategories()
      .then(actions.setBookCategories)
```

```
      .then(dispatch);
  }
}
```

`fetchBooks` takes a category and gets all the books for it from the backend. Then it builds and dispatches the `setBooks` action to update the state with these books.

```
function fetchBooks(category){
  return function(dispatch){
    return api.fetchBooks(category)
      .then(actions.setBooks)
      .then(dispatch);
  }
}

export { fetchBooks, fetchBookCategories };
```

Fetching Data on Load

We need to fetch data when view pages are loaded.

The useEffect hook utility can help in this case. It allows side-effects in view functions. Data fetching is a side-effect.

`useEffect()` takes a callback function and an optional array of dependencies. When no array of dependencies is provided the callback is called after every render. This may be unnecessary in some cases. When an array of dependencies is provided the effect callback is called when one of its dependencies changes. When an empty array is provided the callback is called only once.

The DOM has been updated by the time the effect runs.

Consider the following code running the `fetchBooks(category)` function.

```
useEffect(() => {
    fetchBooks(category);
  },[category]);
```

`useEffect` runs the fetch only when the `category` property changes.

The `Books` view page loads the best selling books when the page is loaded.

```
import React, {useEffect} from 'react';
```

```
import { connect } from 'react-redux';
import { Link } from 'react-router-dom';
import BookList from './BookList';
import { fetchBooks } from './operations';

function Books({match, fetchBooks}){
  const {category} = match.params;

  useEffect(() => {
    fetchBooks(category);
  },[category]);

  return (
    <div>
      <Link to="/">Home</Link>
      <BookList />
    </div>
  )
}

export default connect(null, {fetchBooks})(Books);
```

The view page can access the parameters passed by the routing system using the `match.params` object available in `props`.

Higher-Order Components

The `useEffect()` hook makes view functions impure. We can, however, extract out the impure code from the view.

A higher-order component is a function that takes a component as input and returns a new component.

Higher-order components are a pattern for code reuse. They provide a way to encapsulate the impure code, like data fetching or dispatching an action.

The `connect` utility function is a higher-order component. We can construct a new variation of it that takes an action creator as additional input and builds a component dispatching an action, created with the action creator, when is loaded.

```
import React, {useEffect} from 'react';
```

```
import { connect } from 'react-redux';

function connectWithOnLoad(
    mapState,
    mapDispatch,
    createOnLoadAction) {
    return !createOnLoadAction
      ? connect(mapState, mapDispatch)
      : function(Component){
        return connect(mapState, mapDispatch)(function(props){
            const {dispatch} = props;

            useEffect(() => {
                const onLoadAction = createOnLoadAction(props);
                dispatch(onLoadAction);
            },[]);

            return <Component {...props} />
        });
    }
}

export default connectWithOnLoad;
```

The `connectWithOnLoad` function takes three functions as arguments. When the action creator is not defined it just returns the result of the original `connect` utility called with `mapState` and `mapDispatch` arguments. Otherwise, it returns a new function getting a component and returning a new component. The return component is connected to the store and dispatches an action when is loaded.

The spread attributes used in `<Component {...props} />` makes it easy to pass all the props to the child component.

`useEffect(() => {},[])` called with an empty array as the second argument runs the callback when the component is loaded.

`connectWithOnLoad` has a similar interface to the original `connect` utility but it allows us to pass as a third argument an action creator.

Below is an example of using the new utility.

The `Categories` view page is connected to the store and the `fetchBookCategories` operation is dispatched when the view is loaded.

```
import connect from '../shared/connectWithOnLoad';
import {fetchBookCategories} from './operations';

function Categories({categories}){}

function mapState({books}){}

export default connect(
    mapState,
    null,
    fetchBookCategories
)(Categories);
```

The `Categories` view is a pure function. The impure part stays in the new `connect()` higher-order component.

Articles

Next, let's look at the articles page.

State

The state is just a list of articles.

```
const initialState = [];
```

Actions

We are going to need one action for updating the articles list.

```
import { createAction } from 'redux-actions';

const setArticles = createAction('SET_ARTICLES');

export {
    setArticles
};
```

View Functions

The `ArticleItem` view function creates the UI for a single article.

```
import React from 'react';

function ArticleItem({article}){
  return (
    <div>
     <div>
       <a
         href={article.url}
         target="_blank"
         rel="noopener noreferrer">
          {article.title}
       </a>
     </div>
     <div>{article.author}</div>
     <div>{article.date}</div>
    </div>
  )
}

export default ArticleItem
```

The Articles view function renders a list of articles.

```
import React from 'react';
import { Link } from 'react-router-dom';
import ArticleItem from './ArticleItem'

function Articles({articles}){
  return (
    <div>
      <div><Link to="/">Home</Link></div>
      <h2>Articles</h2>
      <div>
         { articles.map(article =>
            <ArticleItem
             article={article}
             key={article.id} /> )
         }
      </div>
    </div>
  )
```

}

Update Function

The update function handles the `setArticles` action by updating the state with the new list of articles.

```
import { handleActions } from 'redux-actions';
import * as actions from "./actions";

//updaters
function setArticles(state, action){
  const articles = action.payload;
  return articles;
}

export default handleActions({
    [actions.setArticles]: setArticles
  },
  initialState
);
```

API Utils

The API key is something we may need in all pages, so we can extract it out from the books API and put it in a common shared file.

```
const apiKey = '00000000000000000000000000000000';

function getResults(response){
  return (response && response.data)
    ? response.data.results
    : response;
}

export {
  apiKey,
  getResults
};
```

Now, we can use it to define the `fetchMostPopular()` function that fetches the articles from the NYT API.

```
import axios from 'axios';
import {apiKey, getResults} from '../shared/api-tools';

const baseUrl =
    'https://api.nytimes.com/svc/mostpopular/v2/viewed';

function fetchMostPopular(){
  const url = `${baseUrl}/1.json?api-key=${apiKey}`;
  return axios(url)
    .then(getResults);
}

export default {
  fetchMostPopular
};
```

The `fetchMostPopular()` API util function is impure. We can make the API util functions pure by just creating the request. By doing so the impure part moves into the operation using that request object.

```
function requestMostPopular(){
  const url = `${baseUrl}/1.json?api-key=${apiKey}`;
  return { url };
}

export default {
  requestMostPopular
};
```

Operations

A new operation is required for fetching the data and updating the state.

First, we need a few mapping functions.

The `toArticle` function takes an article retrieved from the backend and converts it into an article object with a nicer set of properties.

```
function toArticle(dto){
  return {
    id: dto.id,
    title: dto.title,
    author: dto.byline,
```

```
    url: dto.url,
    date: dto.published_date
  }
}
```

The `toArticles` function does a similar thing. It takes a list of articles got from the backed and converts them to a list of article objects with a nicer set of properties using the `toArticle` mapping function

```
function toArticles(list){
  return list.map(toArticle);
}
```

The `fetchMostPopularArticles` operation makes an API call to retrieve all the popular articles. Then it transforms the result into a list of articles with a nicer set of properties using the `toArticles` function. After that, it creates and dispatches the `setArticles` action containing the new list of articles.

```
import axios from 'axios';
import api from "./api";
import * as actions from './actions';
import { getResults } from '../shared/api-tools';

function fetchMostPopularArticles(){
  return function(dispatch){
    axios(api.requestMostPopular())
      .then(getResults)
      .then(toArticles)
      .then(actions.setArticles)
      .then(dispatch);
  }
}

export { fetchMostPopularArticles };
```

Connecting

The `Articles` view reads the articles from the store. It dispatches the `fetchMostPopularArticles` operation when the page is loaded using the new `connect` higher-order component.

```
import connect from '../shared/connectWithOnLoad';
```

```
import { fetchMostPopularArticles } from './operations';

function mapState({articles}){
  return {
    articles
  }
}

export default connect(
    mapState,
    null,
    fetchMostPopularArticles
)(Articles);
```

Movie Reviews

In a similar way, we can create the movie reviews page. In this case, we are going to define:

- A state branch: `movieReviews` storing a list
- Actions: `setMoviesReviews`
- View functions: `MovieReviewItem()`, `MovieReviews()`
- Update functions: `setMoviesReviews()`
- API utils: `requestCriticsPicks()`
- Operations: `fetchMoviesCriticsPicks()`

Root Update Function

Taking a modular approach and splitting the state management between three update functions, one for each view page, requires to create the root update function.

```
import { combineReducers } from 'redux';
import booksReducer from './books/reducer';
import articlesReducer from './articles/reducer';
import movieReviewsReducer from './movieReviews/reducer';

export default combineReducers({
  books: booksReducer,
  articles: articlesReducer,
  movieReviews: movieReviewsReducer
});
```

App Router

Navigating between several view pages requires routing. As already said, we are going to use the React Router.

```
npm install --save react-router-dom
```

Entry View

The `Home` view page is the first page displayed by the application. It contains links to all the other pages.

```
import React from 'react';
import { Link } from 'react-router-dom';

function Home(){
  return (
    <div>
     <h2>NYT App</h2>
     <div>
        <Link to="/books/">Books Best Sellers</Link>
     </div>
     <div>
        <Link to="/articles/">Most Popular Articles</Link>
     </div>
     <div>
        <Link to="/moviereviews/">Movie Reviews</Link>
     </div>
    </div>
  )
}

export default Home;
```

AppRouter View

The `AppRouter` view defines all the routes using the `Route` component.

The `path` attribute declares the path used in the URL and the `component` attribute defines the view to be rendered when the route matches the URL.

```
import React from 'react';
```

```
import {BrowserRouter as Router, Route} from 'react-router-dom';
import Home from './Home';
import BookCategories from './books/Categories';
import Books from './books/Books';
import Articles from './articles/Articles';
import MovieReviews from './movieReviews/MovieReviews';

function AppRouter(){
  return (
    <Router>
      <Route exact path="/" component={Home} />
      <Route exact path="/books" component={BookCategories} />
      <Route path="/books/:category/" component={Books} />
      <Route exact path="/articles" component={Articles} />
      <Route exact path="/moviereviews"
             component={MovieReviews} />
    </Router>
  )
}

export default AppRouter;
```

Entry Point

In the index.js file, we are going to use the **AppRouter** as the root view.

```
import React from 'react';
import ReactDOM from 'react-dom';
import { createStore, applyMiddleware } from 'redux';
import { composeWithDevTools } from 'redux-devtools-extension';
import { Provider } from 'react-redux';
import thunk from 'redux-thunk';
import rootReducer from './rootReducer';
import AppRouter from './AppRouter';

const store = createStore(rootReducer, composeWithDevTools(
    applyMiddleware(thunk)
 ));

ReactDOM.render(<Provider store={store}>
    <AppRouter />
```

```
</Provider>,
document.getElementById('root'));
```

Final Thoughts

Routing can be enabled with the React Router library. The view with all the routes can be used as the root view. The `<Link>` component is used to navigate to a route defined using the `<Route>` component.

The `useEffect()` hook runs functions containing side-effects. It makes the view function impure.

A higher-order component is a function that takes a component and returns a new component. It is a way of reusing component logic and encapsulate the impure code.

Chapter 16: Fetch Module

The network request can take some time to return a result and can also fail. We should display a loading message while the network request is in progress and show an error message when the request fails.

The common logic for handling the network request progress and errors can be encapsulated in its own module.

State

The information we need to store is the request status and the error message.

```
const Status = Object.freeze({
  Pending: 'Pending',
  Success: 'Success',
  Failure: 'Failure'
});

const initialState = Object.freeze({
  status: null,
  error: ''
});
```

Actions

We need new actions for marking the start and failure of a network request.

Request/Success/Failure is a pattern used in network requests async actions. It requires actions marking the beginning of the request and actions marking the result of the request.

```
import { createAction } from 'redux-actions';
```

```
const fetchStart = createAction('FETCH_START');
const fetchSuccess = createAction('FETCH_SUCCESS');
const fetchFailure = createAction('FETCH_FAILURE');

export { fetchStart, fetchSuccess, fetchFailure };
```

Selectors

In order to detect if the request is still in progress, we can use a selector.

```
import { Status } from './reducer';

function isLoading(state){
  return state.fetch.status === Status.Pending;
}

export { isLoading };
```

View Functions

The `FetchStatus` view function displays the "Loading ..." text when the request is in progress and the error message when the request fails.

```
import React from 'react';

function FetchStatus({ error, isLoading }){
  return (
    <div>
     <div>
      {isLoading && 'Loading ...'}
     </div>
     <div>
      {error}
     </div>
    </div>
  )
}
```

Connecting

The `FetchStatus` view reads the error message from the store and uses the `isLoading()` selector to set the boolean value deciding the display of the "Loading..." text.

```
import { connect } from 'react-redux';
import { isLoading } from './selectors';

function mapState(state){
  return {
    error: state.fetch.error,
    isLoading: isLoading(state)
  }
}

export default connect(
  mapState
)(FetchStatus)
```

Update Functions

The update function handles the three actions.

When the request starts, the error message is cleared and the status is set to `Status.Pending`.

When the request succeeds, the error message is cleared and the status is set to `Status.Success`.

When the request fails, the error message is set and the status becomes `Status.Failure`.

```
import { handleActions } from 'redux-actions';
import * as actions from './actions';

//updaters
function fetchStart(state, action){
  return {
    status: Status.Pending,
    error: ''
  }
}
```

```
function fetchFailure(state, action){
  const { message } = action.payload;
  return {
    status: Status.Failure,
    error: message
  }
}

function fetchSuccess(state, action){
  return {
    status: Status.Success,
    error: ''
  }
}

export default handleActions({
    [actions.fetchStart]: fetchStart,
    [actions.fetchSuccess]: fetchSuccess,
    [actions.fetchFailure]: fetchFailure
  },
  initialState
);
```

Operations

When the request starts, the `fetchStart` action is dispatched. If the request succeeds, the `fetchSuccess` action is dispatched. If the request fails, the `fetchFailure` action is dispatched with the error message.

We can create an operation that encapsulates the code making the network request and dispatching these actions.

```
import axios from 'axios';
import {fetchStart, fetchSuccess, fetchFailure} from './actions';

function getResults(response){
  return (response && response.data)
    ? response.data.results
    : response;
}
```

```
function fetch(request){
  return function(dispatch){
    dispatch(fetchStart())
    return axios(request)
      .then(getResults)
      .then(function success(data){
        dispatch(fetchSuccess());
        return data;
      })
      .catch(function handlerError(error){
        dispatch(fetchFailure(error));
        throw error;
      });
  }
}

export { fetch };
```

NYT with the Fetch Module

Let's integrate the Fetch Module in the NYT application.

Views

The `FetchStatus` view can simply be imported and used in any view showing data from a network request. Here is an example of using the `FetchStatus` view in the `Articles` view:

```
import React from 'react';
import FetchStatus from '../fetch/FetchStatus';

function Articles({articles}){
  return (
    <div>
      <div><Link to="/">Home</Link></div>
      <h2>Articles</h2>
      <FetchStatus />
      ...
    </div>
  )
}
```

Operations

The shared fetch operation can simplify the network requests in other operations. Consider the code below using the fetch operation to request the most popular articles and dispatching the `fetchStart`, `fetchSuccess` and `fetchFailure` actions.

```
import api from "./api";
import * as actions from './actions';
import { fetch } from '../fetch/operations';

function fetchMostPopularArticles(){
  return function(dispatch){
    dispatch(fetch(api.requestMostPopular()))
      .then(toArticles)
      .then(actions.setArticles)
      .then(dispatch);
  }
}
```

Root Update Function

With `combineReducer()` we create the root update function.

```
import { combineReducers } from 'redux';
import articlesReducer from './articles/reducer';
import fetchReducer from './fetch/reducer';
...

export default combineReducers({
    articles: articlesReducer,
    fetch: fetchReducer,
    ...
});
```

Final Thoughts

The Request/Success/Failure pattern uses actions for marking the beginning and the result of a request.

A shared operation making the network call and dispatching `Request`, `Success` and `Failure` actions can simplify the creation of specific operations doing network requests.

Modules can encapsulate common logic that can be reused in other places.

Chapter 17: Functional Architecture with React and Redux

The two fundamental concepts in functional programming are immutable data and pure functions.

For the most part, functional programming is about transformations of immutable data. We can think about these transformations as mapping inputs to outputs without any side-effects.

- View functions transform props into UI
- Update functions transform the state into a new state
- Actions creators transform values into plain actions objects
- API request util functions transform values into plain request objects
- Higher-order components transform components into other components

Decomposition

Functional programming guides the decomposition of the application into small functions, which are then combined together.

The root view is split in smaller views and thus making the tree of views.

The root state is decomposed in branches and thus making the state tree.

The root update function is decomposed into smaller update functions and thus making the tree of update functions.

When mapping the state branches to update functions, combineReducers() can be used to split the root update function into smaller update functions.

When mapping actions to an update function, handleActions() can be used to split it into even smaller update functions.

Here is a sketch of the unidirectional flow pointing out the tree structures.

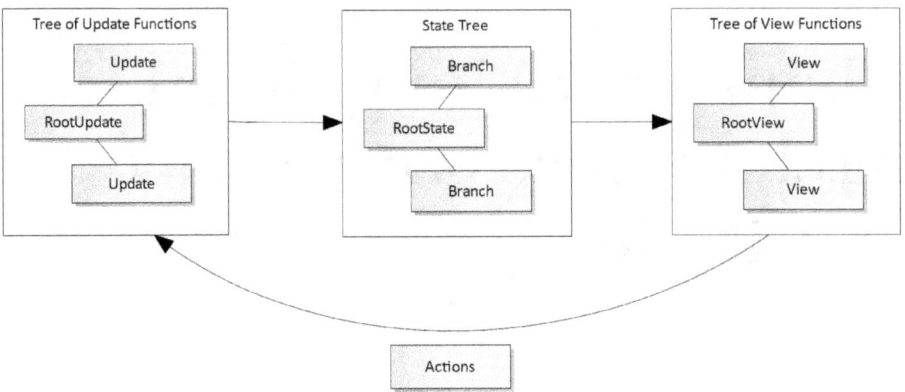

When the application starts, it wires up only the root view with the root update function.

In an application with routing, each view page has its own tree of views.

Purity

Update functions, selectors, action creators are pure functions. Even the API util functions can become pure by just creating the request objects.

We are aiming to make view functions as pure functions.

Even if the application does reads and writes to the DOM, and changes the state, the unidirectional data flow allows writing only pure functions. The impure part is handle by React and Redux. React uses the pure view functions to create the UI and listen to user interactions. Redux uses pure update functions to change the state.

Pure functions treat inputs as immutable values. Changing immutable values means creating changed copies. The simplest way to work with immutable values is to freeze objects at creation and to use the spread operator for copying objects.

Side-Effects

Side-effects are express by the interaction with the outside world, like network requests or sending timer events. Any asynchronous logic is a side-effect.

We need to minimize the number of side-effects and encapsulate them.

Asynchronous action creators are functions returning functions. These functions called operations, or thunk actions are the main place for encapsulating side-effects. Thunk actions can dispatch other thunk actions or standard plain actions.

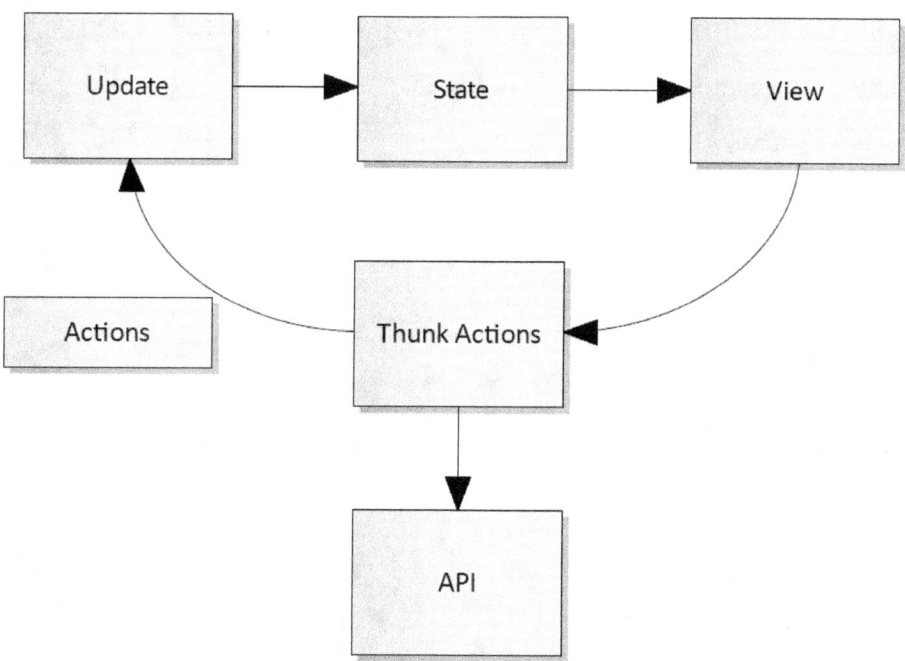

Impure View Functions

The two main hooks for managing side-effects inside view functions are `useState()` and `useEffect()`.

When building reusable view functions with their own UI state, like the `ShowMore` component, the local state is a better alternative than having the state in the store. That means using the `useState()` hook in the view.

Side-effects should go mainly into thunk actions. If we are going to use the `useEffect()` hook, it should be just to dispatch thunk actions. Even better we can encapsulate this dispatch logic into higher-order components.

Folder Structure

The feature-first approach is a good way to structure folders in an application. As the app grows and more features are needed, we add more folders.

Feature-first means that the top-level folders are named after the main features. For example `books`, `articles`, `movies`, `fetch`.

This approach means having view files and update files related to the same feature in the same folder. Each feature comes with its folder.

Here is an example of a feature folder:

```
feature_name/
|-- actions.js
|-- reducers.js
|-- reducers.test.js
|-- selectors.js
|-- api.js
|-- operations.js
|-- View.jsx
```

Below is a sample of the folder structure for the NYT app.

```
articles/
|-- actions.js
|-- reducers.js
|-- api.js
|-- operations.js
|-- ArticleItem.jsx
|-- Articles.jsx
books/
|-- actions.js
|-- reducers.js
|-- api.js
|-- operations.js
|-- BookItem.jsx
|-- BookList.jsx
|-- Books.jsx
|-- CategoryItem.jsx
|-- Categories.jsx
fetch/
|-- actions.js
```

```
|-- reducers.js
|-- selectors.js
|-- operations.js
|-- FetchStatus.jsx
movieReviews/
|-- ...
```

Common functionalities like `fetch` come also with their own folder.

Final Thoughts

The focus in functional programming is on pure functions and immutable values. Functions transform immutable data.

The main point is to create applications that are easier to reason about. We are going to achieve this by creating small, well-named pure functions and then combine them in a functional way, and by using immutable values to transfer data between those functions.

The entire application state is an immutable tree structure managed by a single store. The UI is decomposed in view functions that connect to the store and transform part of the state into a visual interface. The user interaction is expressed by dispatching actions. Actions are handled by pure update functions. Update functions take the current state and an action and return a new state. The new state is then passed again to the view functions.

What's next?

For a more in-depth look at JavaScript and main functional principles, you may read 'Discover Functional JavaScript'. Here, you will find more on pure functions, immutability, currying, decorators but also ideas on how to make code easier to read. JavaScript brings functional programming to the mainstream and offers a new way of doing object-oriented programming without classes and prototypes.

In the 'Functional Programming in JavaScript' book you will find how to use JavaScript as a functional programming language by disabling the 'this' keyword and enforcing immutable objects with a linter. You will learn how to use statements like 'if' and 'switch' in a functional way, or how to create and use functors and monads. It turns out that JavaScript has everything it needs to be used as a functional language. We just have to remove features from the language.

If you want to learn how to build modern React applications using functional components and functional programming principles, you can consider reading 'Functional React, 2nd Edition'.

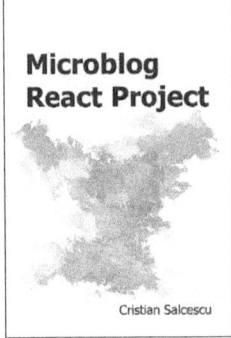

The 'Microblog React Project' book takes a project-based learning approach by engaging you in building a practical application. The reader will learn things on the way by developing different parts of this project. The Microblog application will be built using React with Hooks and libraries like Redux, Redux Thunk, Redux Toolkit, Material UI, or Axios.

The 'UI State Management' book gives you an overview of how state is managed by building a note-taking application with four different libraries. We start from an object-oriented approach using Svelte, centralize state with Vuex, then move to a functional approach with React and Redux, and in the end arrive at a solution using only pure functions with Elm.

The Composition API provides a new way of managing reactivity. It is made of a set of Reactive API functions plus the facility to register lifecycle hooks. Understand better the reactivity system by building one from scratch and then implement a master-details functionality. Check how to manage state using the Composition API and then use it to implement a central store similar to Vuex.

Enjoy the learning journey!

About the author

Cristian Salcescu is the author of Functional React.
He is a Technical Lead passionate about front-end development and enthusiastic about sharing ideas. He took different roles and participated in all parts of software creation.
Cristian Salcescu is a JavaScript trainer and a writer on Medium.

www.ingramcontent.com/pod-product-compliance
Lightning Source LLC
Chambersburg PA
CBHW071409210526
45465CB00001B/314